This book is dedicated to those men and women who have served in the armed forces. During the American Civil War, the veterans who survived the horrors of that conflict had a saying ... *"I've seen the elephant,"* simply meaning that they have seen combat and lived to talk about it. For those of you who have served or are currently serving, we thank you for your dedication to your country. And for those brave soldiers who gave their *last full measure,* we salute you! This is your book!

Patrick Burke

As president of American Battlefield Ghost Hunters Society, Patrick Burke has spent years building his network and career as a renowned paranormal expert. His efforts in the area of haunted battlefield research have paved the way to a better understanding of the nature of warfare and its relationship to paranormal phenomena. Based on his knowledge and experience, he has been invited as a presenter and teacher to several paranormal conferences and events. His first book, *Battlefield Guide to Ghost Hunting,* has become a great resource for those interested in conducting paranormal field research.

Jack Roth

Jack Roth is a veteran writer and investigative journalist who has spent the last eighteen years investigating and researching paranormal phenomena. His innate curiosity and attention to detail have helped him develop an extensive network of contacts in the world of paranormal studies. He also has spent countless hours organizing and leading excursions to haunted locations in an effort to introduce others to paranormal field research. In the process, he has learned a great deal about the nature of hauntings—as well as documenting and evaluating evidence—from world-renowned experts in the field.

To Write to the Authors

If you wish to contact the author or would like more information about this book, please write to the author in care of Llewellyn Worldwide, and we will forward your request. Both author and publisher appreciate hearing from you and learning of your enjoyment of this book and how it has helped you. Llewellyn Worldwide cannot guarantee that every letter written to the author can be answered, but all will be forwarded. Please write to:

℅ Llewellyn Worldwide
2143 Wooddale Drive
Woodbury, MN 55125-2989

Please enclose a self-addressed stamped envelope for reply,
or $1.00 to cover costs. If outside the USA, enclose
an international postal reply coupon.

Many of Llewellyn's authors have websites with additional information and resources. For more information, please visit us at: www.llewellyn.com.

Searching for Spirits on
America's Most Famous Battlefield

GHOST
SOLDIERS

of

Gettysburg

PATRICK BURKE
JACK ROTH

Llewellyn Worldwide
Woodbury, Minnesota

FIRST EDITION
First Printing, 2014

Book design by Bob Gaul
Cover art © iStockphoto.com/26709028/©Geoff Kuchera
            iStockphoto.com/4998450/©DenGuy
Cover design by Lisa Novak
Editing by Ed Day
Interior photos courtesy of the Library of Congress, Jack Roth, and Debbie Estep

DISCLAIMER: Some of the names in this book have been changed in order to protect the privacy of the witness.

Llewellyn Publications is a registered trademark of Llewellyn Worldwide Ltd.

Library of Congress Cataloging-in-Publication Data
Burke, Patrick.
  Ghost soldiers of Gettysburg: searching for spirits on America's most famous battle-field/Patrick Burke, Jack Roth.—First Edition.
     pages cm
  ISBN 978-0-7387-3970-0
1. Ghosts—Pennsylvania—Gettysburg National Military Park. 2. Haunted places—Pennsylvania—Gettysburg. 3. Gettysburg, Battle of, Gettysburg, Pa., 1863—Miscellanea. I. Title.
  BF1472.U6R676 2014
  133.1'2974842—dc23
                        2014020479

Llewellyn Publications
A Division of Llewellyn Worldwide Ltd.
2143 Wooddale Drive
Woodbury, MN 55125-2989
www.llewellyn.com

Printed in the United States of America

Contents

Day One: July 1, 1863 ... 41

Day Two: July 2, 1863 ... 77

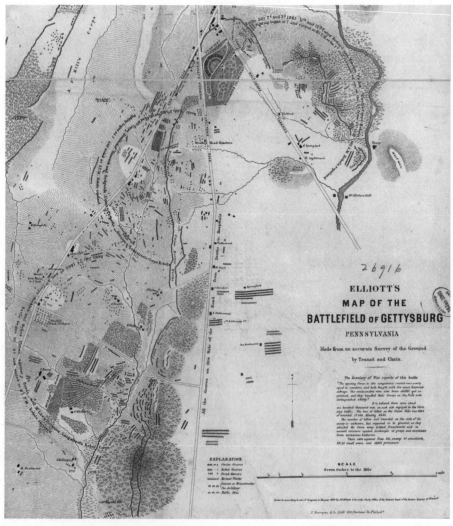

*This map was created in 1864 by S. G. Elliott & Co. and shows
the entire battlefield at Gettysburg in 1863. Its details include
Union and Rebel graves, dead horses, and rifle pits.*

**Note: This map has been cropped; please see Elliot's Map of the Battlefield
of Gettysburg courtesy the Library of Congress for the full-size image.*
(http://www.loc.gov/item/99447500)

Acknowledgments

— Patrick Burke —

To my wonderful wife, Jean, for her ongoing support and belief in all that I do, you are the best part of my life! To my daughters, Emily and Shannon, who in their own right are becoming talented sensitives and paranormal investigators, you both are the light of my life. This book, on my part, is also dedicated to my brother John, who has crossed the great beyond and is still telling me where to point the camera! To those brave souls who have ventured forth with me on many a battlefield—Mike Hartness, Darryl Smith, Jack Roth, Mary Burke-Russell, Melody Hood Bussey, Terry Templaski, Richard Flaum, Susan Eshleman, Peggy Cole, Andrew Dodson, Harry Grant, Chris Carouthers, and Karen Mitchell and so many others— this book is also for you. And for all of the men who gave their last full measure, regardless of what war or conflict, I thank you for your service.

— Jack Roth —

I want to thank all of my friends and family members who have supported my research endeavors over the years. I especially want to thank Dr. Andrew Nichols, who has not only been a true mentor to me, but a dear friend. I also want to thank Scott Flagg, with whom I've shared many profound paranormal experiences and enjoyed traveling around the country. A huge thanks to my wife, Lisa, whose patience and understanding have allowed me to pursue my dreams with clarity of mind. And finally, a big thank you to my son, Nathaniel, whose open-minded curiosity to all things mysterious constantly reminds me that searching for the truth is not only a worthwhile cause, but also a freedom that is our birthright. And finally, to the brave individuals who fought at the Battle of Gettysburg, I honor your courage and sacrifice.

Foreword

— by Dr. Andrew Nichols —
Executive Director, American Institute
of Parapsychology, author of *Ghost Detective:
Adventures of a Parapsychologist*

Military battles are among the most tragic and traumatizing of human events, and it is just such events that often result in the formation of a "haunted atmosphere." The Battle of Gettysburg was certainly the bloodiest encounter of the American Civil War, and it is regarded as the turning point in the conflict that divided our nation. Thus, we should not be surprised that this battlefield in Pennsylvania has acquired a reputation for being one of the most haunted sites in the United States, if not the entire world.

Spiritualists believe that ghosts are earthbound spirits of dead people; that after death our spirits continue to exist in another dimension, but that some spirits—often in cases of sudden or violent death—become attached to a certain location where they can sometimes be seen, heard, or felt by certain people. Evidence suggests that this explanation is inadequate for many ghostly appearances. The majority of ghosts are almost certainly subjective; they have no objective reality outside the minds of those who experience them. Skeptics assert that all such experiences are hallucinations, dreams, or figments of the imagination, and that is the complete answer to the question of ghosts. Many reported apparitions can indeed be explained in this way, but it is not as simple as that.

The majority of parapsychologists, myself among them, believe that many ghosts are a type of telepathic image, created at some time during the past by a living mind during a period of extreme stress. Such a telepathic residue might remain for many years, available to anyone who is sufficiently endowed with the capacity for extrasensory perception (ESP). Research suggests that about 15 to 20 percent of the population is psychically sensitive enough to experience an apparition. This "psychic residue" theory is only that—a theory. As yet, it cannot be proved. It is a theory that could account for many ghosts, but certainly not all of them. However, it would also explain why most haunting apparitions seem to fade away after a number of years, as the telepathic image, like a depleted battery, gradually loses its "charge."

The honest answer to the question "What are ghosts?" is that we don't know. We do know that people experience ghosts. They can be seen, heard, or felt by certain people. Methodical, responsible, and honest ghost hunters can contribute much to our understanding of these mysterious phenomena, and with the help of dedicated researchers such as the authors of this book, I believe we will one day know what ghosts actually are and why they appear.

When I began my own investigations in the field of psychical research more than thirty-five years ago, ghost hunting was a pastime restricted to spiritualists, eccentrics, and a few isolated scholars. Today, a large number of serious, well-trained enthusiasts are actively engaged in the study of paranormal phenomena. My friend and colleague, Jack Roth, along with his co-author Patrick Burke, are among those who have established themselves as dedicated professional paranormal investigators.

I know Patrick through his fine reputation as a researcher and field investigator, and my friendship and professional relationship with Jack spans nearly two decades. Together, Jack and I have investigated numerous reports of hauntings over the years, and his dedication, enthusiasm, and insight have been a source of inspiration for me. I can think of no one better suited to present the *Ghost Soldiers of Gettysburg*.

With this book, the two authors have provided us with a substantial contribution to psychical research; a study of one of the most intriguing and controversial of paranormal events—the ancient enigma of haunted battlefields. Whether or not you are already a believer in ghosts—or consider yourself a skeptic—no doubt you will be fascinated by this vivid and engaging account of their explorations on the frontiers of scientific knowledge.

Preface

Some of the most vicious hand-to-hand fighting that took place during the Battle of Gettysburg occurred at East Cemetery Hill. It was a cold night and the wind was picking up as we headed down toward the base of the hill to stand on Wainwright Avenue, formerly known as Brickyard Road. Patrick stood just to the left of the Seventh West Virginia Infantry marker. John, his brother, stood against the guardrail looking down where the Confederates from Hokes Brigade would have formed lines for their charge up the hill to silence and seize the guns that had been blasting away at them for hours. Jack was standing behind Patrick, where one of the Union rifle pits would have been. Jack, a Floridian, commented on the cold and worried that the wind was killing any chance of capturing quality electronic voice phenomena (EVP). Suddenly... "They're here," said John. He coughed and asked the Confederate boys to give us a rebel yell.

With the wind whipping around us, we knew we would be able to capture video with the infrared camcorder Patrick was holding, but audio was going to be worthless... and that's when it happened. John laughed and pointed towards the thin woods at the base of Cemetery Hill. "Here they come," he said. As a sensitive, John was good at seeing the shadows of the ghost soldiers, so when he said "over here," we inevitably rushed to the location he was referring to with great results. Patrick turned his head to look down into the area where John was pointing and saw a flash of light. Then he felt a wave of emotion wash over him. Jack, sensing something strange was happening, whispered, "Here we go."

Suddenly, the wind stopped, as if all sound had frozen in time. Patrick saw a mass of blackness surging up to his left. He focused his camera on the area the anomaly would pass through in hopes of capturing the event. And then it was over. The ambient sound came back, and the wind started blowing even more fiercely than before the phenomenon took place.

Afterward we tried to describe what we had felt. The consensus was that the mass of black energy had carried with it every emotion one could imagine when men are gripped in mortal combat. Patrick described it as fury, tinged with the fear of knowing you were most likely going to die, but you push forward anyway. John described it as a madness that consumed the human soul, and Jack described it as fear and hopelessness all rolled up into one.

Upon reviewing the infrared tape, we were amazed at what we captured. At the very moment the wind died down, a shadow passed between the camera and the tree it was focused on. And then one of the most incredible sounds we have ever heard on a battlefield became clearly audible . . . the death wail. It can only be described as a soul screaming out in rage at the inevitability of its bodily death. It sounded as if a whole chorus of voices was crying out in frustration as they faced the moment of their violent demise. Incredible. But this was Gettysburg, so we weren't surprised in the least.

Introduction

Historically, Gettysburg is one of the most significant battles fought during the American Civil War. In June 1863, Gen. Robert E. Lee marched his Army of Northern Virginia into the Union stronghold of Pennsylvania and over the first three days of July, the Union Army of the Potomac met the Confederate invaders and defeated them at a small town called Gettysburg. It is seen as the great turning point in the Civil War. Most historians agree that from a strategic standpoint, Gettysburg was the Confederacy's last chance at victory.

By spring 1863, the Confederate task was becoming increasingly difficult. One of the reasons Lee invaded the North was to ease the strain on Southern resources. Almost the entire war had been fought on Southern soil, which had taken a financial and physical toll on the Confederate states. Lee also believed that another crushing Union defeat, especially on Northern soil, might force President Abraham Lincoln to end the war and leave the Confederacy alone. Add to this the possible benefits a Confederate victory could have in persuading both Great Britain and France to recognize, and support, a new Southern nation, and the benefits seemed to outweigh the risks. In reality, however, the fate of the Confederacy hung in the balance.

The enormity of the battle and the absolute devastation it inflicted on human life cannot be overstated. In 1860, Gettysburg was a small town of about 2,400 citizens. For three hot, humid days in July 1863, two huge armies came crashing on top of them. Eighty-two thousand Union soldiers and 75,000 Confederates pounded into each other like two freight trains. The thought of 157,000 American soldiers having at each other in a town of 2,400 people is hard to imagine. When the fighting was over, approximately 51,000 of these soldiers were casualties. Of this number, 7,058 died in combat, 33,264 were wounded and of those wounded at least a quarter of them died from medical complications. Add to this 10,790 soldiers who were either captured or declared missing in action, and you're left with unimaginable carnage. This represented the largest number of casualties in any battle of an already-bloody war—a casualty rate of more than 32 percent! The total American population in 1863 was only 31 million, which makes the percentage of households affected by this one battle staggering.

Gettysburg took on an even greater mythical quality when President Lincoln decided to accept an invitation to speak at the dedication of a cemetery for many of the soldiers killed in the battle. During this ceremony, Lincoln delivered his famous Gettysburg Address. His speech, considered one of the most brilliant by any statesman in history, resonated with hope and national unity at a time when people were numb from the death and destruction secession had brought. Lincoln's words read like poetry with phrases such as "conceived in liberty" and "all men are created equal." Perhaps the most stirring part resides in the words "that government of the people, by the people, for the people, shall not perish from the earth." Lincoln's brilliant speech made the battle even more significant historically, as both continue to define the broader, philosophical meaning of separation, suffering, and reunion.

*In three days of fighting, there were more than 51,000 casualties
at the Battle of Gettysburg. Courtesy of the Library of Congress.*

All of these factors add up to Gettysburg representing the perfect
environment in which to conduct paranormal field research. The overwhelming number of documented paranormal experiences in Gettysburg
suggests that, as Gov. Joshua Lawrence Chamberlain, a Civil War general,
eloquently stated in his dedication speech to the Maine monuments in
1888, something does stay and spirits do in fact linger. Even when we use
critical, objective, scientific reasoning to discount the majority of these
experiences as misinterpretations of normal events, a wealth of compelling, corroborative, verifiable evidence remains, including scientific data
and video, still photographs, electronic sound recordings, and first- and
second-hand eyewitness testimony from our investigations alone.

We knew that focusing our attention on Gettysburg would give us the
best chance of validating the haunting experience and prove that the soul,

or at least a part of human consciousness, survives bodily death. Research has shown that there's a higher percentage of paranormal activity at locations where emotions ran high and trauma was involved, which makes battlefields great places to conduct paranormal research.

Gettysburg is replete with ghost stories. Tens of thousands of visitors, as well as people who live in Gettysburg and around the battlefield, have had their own personal ghostly encounters with the ghost soldiers who still reside there. Gettysburg is a well-documented paranormal vortex. Everything from harrowing firsthand accounts to hard data—still photographs of apparitions, videos of walking ghost soldiers, the captured voices of the dead, and other paranormal activity—make Gettysburg the perfect location to explore haunted history.

Patrick's Story

When I was fifteen, my mom and I spent the entire summer at our second home in St. Mary's County, Maryland. There wasn't a whole lot to do there, but a friend of my parents, known to me as Colonel Boyer, a venerable older gentleman who served through both World Wars, got hold of me when he found out I was in town and asked if I could help unpack and organize some of his books, which were too heavy for him to heft around. So of course I agreed.

The Colonel's book collection was outstanding—every book you could imagine written on military history was there. During the second week of organizing, I came across a box that was tucked away in a corner. The books inside had that musty, haven't-been-read-in-a-long-time smell. I picked up the first book and discovered the wonderful world of Official Reports of the Battle of Gettysburg, and that summer I read the entire book of reports, which were written by Union and Confederate commanders who participated in the battle. I've been hooked on history—especially military history—ever since.

Once I became interested in investigating haunted phenomena, I decided to follow my heart and focus on battlefields. There are several reasons for this. First and foremost, William Tecumseh Sherman, a well-remembered Union general, once stated simply, "War is hell." If you accept this description as accurate and apply it to certain theories associated with paranormal phenomena, then battlefields represent the most likely places on which to capture paranormal evidence due to their association with profoundly traumatic events. In a haunted house, you're usually dealing with strong emotions manifested by one or maybe dozens of people over several decades. On battlefields, unspeakable and horrific emotions emanated from thousands of men in a very short period of time. The bottom line, as Jack likes to say, is that "battlefields can't be matched from an emotional intensity standpoint, and as such they represent the best 'outdoor laboratories' paranormal investigators have at their disposal to conduct valuable field research."

Another reason, perhaps stemming from a deeper spiritual urge as a sensitive to spirits, is that I honestly feel drawn to these ghost soldiers. The heroic and unfortunate souls who sacrificed everything on battlefields across the globe have stories to tell, and I want to share these stories with others in honor of their sacrifices. When visiting battlefields, I often wonder to myself, "What was it like fighting on this particular spot for these boys?" and "What horrors did they endure while trying to act courageously and survive at the same time?" For whatever reason, I feel compelled to know these things…maybe because we owe it to them in some way… to understand, no matter how sad or painful that knowledge might be.

When I first visited Gettysburg as a young teenager, I was walking around the popular places with my friends from school when I had my first paranormal experience on a battlefield. Standing at the top of Little Round Top and looking down into the Valley of Death, I could see Devil's Den. I asked aloud to my friend standing with me, "What was it like fighting here?" and I heard a deep voice say, "Hell!" I looked at my friend and asked if he said something. He shook his head "no" and walked off to catch up with our friends, leaving me standing alone, wondering who could have answered my question.

The next time I went to Gettysburg was in 2000 to conduct my first paranormal investigation, and since that night I've visited the battlefield two to three times a year. Over the course of those visits, I've had incredible experiences and gathered some amazing verifiable evidence. I discovered at a young age that I was a sensitive, one of those people who could see, hear, and communicate with those who have left their mortal bodies behind. I didn't really pursue developing my psychic abilities until I got out of the military years later.

Now when I go to Gettysburg, it's like a reunion for me. I feel like the ghost soldiers know who I am and know that I'm simply trying to capture a bit of their story, what I call "history through the eyes of the participants." There have been certain spirits who wanted to "cross over," and I've helped facilitate that process for them. Sometimes when I go back to areas like The Triangular Field, Bliss Farm, or Cemetery Ridge, some of these ghost soldiers pop in just to say "hey." For me, Gettysburg holds a fascination that's hard to explain. There will always be a part of me that resides there.

Jack's Story

From the time I was a little boy, I've been fascinated with the American Civil War. In fact, when I was six years old, I remember my mom taking me to the library to check out the same book over and over again—*American Heritage Battle Maps of the Civil War*. The maps created by David Greenspan in this particular collection captured my imagination, as I envisioned how incredible it must have been to live in that critical time in American history and fight in such grand battles. As I grew older and the realities of war became clearer to me, I still longed to know what it must have been like, but with a keener sense of the horrifying and senseless nature of warfare.

In 1995, I had an experience at a haunted plantation in Louisiana that changed my life and catapulted me into the world of paranormal research. As I learned about the nature of hauntings and how to properly investigate historic locations, I began to understand more about the human condition. History, after all, is a reflection of humanity, and it became apparent to me that emotional imprints remain wherever strong human emotions were experienced. Whether in a house where a murder was committed, an orphanage where children were abused, or a battlefield where men were violently massacred, it's always the same. Something lingers—an energy, a feeling, a spirit—that tells us something about the people who were there at specific moments in time.

For me, Gettysburg represents the ultimate haunted location due to the man-made maelstrom that was perpetrated there during three days of carnage in July 1863. Excruciating pain, suffering, sorrow, hopelessness, sadness, paralyzing fear, and death overwhelmed that small Pennsylvania town and surrounding battlefield, scorching every inch of it with an emotional residue that remains there to this day.

I feel fortunate to have spent time in Gettysburg over the years, immersing myself in its history and searching within it for answers to some of life's most perplexing mysteries. From a paranormal research standpoint, it's a perfect field laboratory. From a personal standpoint, I've been touched by phenomena that still escape rational explanation, and I've grown as a person and expanded my perception of reality because of it. But mostly, I continue to be humbled by what more than 150,000 men experienced there in 1863 . . . humbled by their sense of duty and sacrifice. When it comes to Gettysburg, nothing has changed much since I was a little boy. My curiosity still drives me to understand more about what it must have been like for these men. Thankfully, as a result of the energies and emotions that still linger there, I feel like I've been able to catch glimpses of the past, and to know, at least partially, what it must have been like for those who experienced it.

———————

When we met at a conference some years ago at Gettysburg, we immediately knew that we were kindred spirits. We talked all night and into the early hours of the morning with a group of friends and associates. It soon became apparent, as one of our mutual friends and researchers pointed out, that we viewed the area of battlefield paranormal research from the same perspective. Add to that our mutual love of all things historic, and a fast friendship developed.

At that conference, we had a chance to talk about our various theories and techniques for investigating battlefield hauntings. By the end of the conference, we agreed that attempting to communicate with the ghost soldiers, as well as experiencing the strong residual energies associated with battlefields, gave us a unique and very rare opportunity to "touch history." We believe these anomalies act as time machines, enabling us to transcend time and space in order to touch the past.

We also strongly believe that we can capture, and validate with the help of science, a genuine historic moment in time. We also feel that we can more accurately predict when paranormal phenomena might manifest by amassing a library of data that include details of the various conditions typically present before, during, and after the paranormal event occurs. By studying the patterns associated with ghostly phenomena, we feel it increases our chances of being at the right place at the right time; a luxury that field investigators don't usually enjoy.

With the writing of this book, our goal is to bring these historic moments to life and give readers the opportunity to experience living history through the eyes of both eyewitnesses to paranormal events and the actual participants of the battle! *Ghost Soldiers of Gettysburg* is a collection of experiences, many of which can be supported by verifiable evidence and further validated by modern-day scientific theories. By using various electronic devices, such as EMF detectors and natural tri-field meters to gauge the electromagnetic field fluctuations; setting up infrared video camcorders in strategic locations; and taking still photos of the environment with both digital and 35mm cameras, we can best capture the kind of tangible evidence required to satisfy the scientific method. We also use digital audio recorders to capture the voices of ghost soldiers and utilize a method of capturing these voices with a technique called "The Double-Blind Ghost Box," developed by our good friends Shawn Taylor and Dan Morgan.

Based on our experiences, we feel it is just as important to acknowledge the benefit of having sensitives (aka mediums) on the team. People with the ability to recognize potential locations that are more prone to paranormal activity, and sensitives can help field investigators determine where to set up equipment and focus their attention. By bringing along those who possess a heightened awareness of the spirit world and who sometimes have the ability to communicate with the spirits of fallen soldiers, we dramatically increase our capture rate in regards to ghostly activity. Our documented evidence includes photographs and video recordings of apparitions and shadow walkers, sound recordings of discarnate voices and the sound of battle, and measured changes in both temperature and electromagnetic fields in the environment.

From a research standpoint, we always start with the history of the battle. By knowing everything about the regiments that fought in a particular area, we not only obtain a clearer picture of the events that took place, but we can also attempt to communicate with the ghost soldiers on a more intimate level. Our research takes us to the individual men in the company. By reading their diaries and the letters they sent home, we gain a better understanding of their everyday lives as soldiers, as well as the intimate details associated with their strongest emotions felt in the heat of battle.

The book is written in an easy-to-understand format. Each day of the battle is separated into parts that begin with a brief description of what occurred that day. This is followed in chapter format by the stories associated with that particular day. Each story is also set by specific location. We did this so that those of you who aren't familiar with the details of the battle can easily follow the stories as they progress through the actual phases of the conflict. We also did this so that those of you who are brave enough can go to the locations where the paranormal events occurred and perhaps encounter the ghost soldiers for yourself.

Our ultimate goal for this book is to share the evidence we've accumulated over the years in order to provide people with a better understanding of not only paranormal phenomena, but of the hardships and horrors tens of thousands of soldiers—many merely boys—experienced when they fought at Gettysburg for three days in July 1863. After all, they deserve to have their stories told.

Chapter One

Overview of Paranormal Phenomena

This book focuses on the field research we have conducted on the Gettysburg battlefield. Our experiences support the idea that the best locations to collect evidence of ghostly activity are those where extreme violence and suffering has occurred. Unfortunately, the human tendency to search for spiritual enlightenment isn't the only thing that has prevailed since the dawn of primitive cultures; our inclination toward violence and conquering others shares this dubious honor. As a result, a plethora of battlegrounds dot the surface of our planet. Nevertheless, if you're interested in ghosts and plan to visit a battlefield someday, you need to know what to look for. Before you can understand the nature of an experience, you must first ask an essential question: What exactly is a ghost?

One of the first things a paranormal field investigator learns is that a ghost isn't so simple to define. Many factors can cause a house or battleground to be haunted, and supernatural episodes are fairly diverse in nature. Wise men often declare that knowledge is power, and in the case of ghosts this is quite true. The best way to fight the fear of the unknown is to embrace and understand it. By properly discerning what you're dealing with, you'll be better equipped to confront it objectively, regardless of how scary it may seem on the surface. This is sage advice for paranormal researchers, who deal with potentially frightening situations all the time. Having said this, battlefield haunts tend to come in several guises.

Parapsychologists and researchers who remain open-minded enough to believe in such possibilities tend to define a ghost as an electromagnetic energy field containing a fragment of consciousness—or personality—of someone who has died tragically or traumatically. At the moment of death, the separation between the physical body and personality (soul) is hampered by a condition of emotional shock that prevents normal transition to the spirit world. As a result, the condition of death isn't recorded in the conscious mind of the one who has died. Life as it was continues to exist in the mind of the deceased, and the personality to whom this occurs is unable to recognize reality. This is referred to as a genuine, or intelligent, haunting.

Some parapsychologists believe genuine hauntings account for only a small percentage of ghostly phenomena and actually represent a telepathic connection between the minds of the deceased and the living witnesses. Physicality has been removed from the equation, so the witnesses aren't really seeing or hearing anything in a physical sense. This theory remains highly debatable, as finding the cause of this telepathic link still eludes the most ardent researchers.

An example of a genuine haunting might play out in this manner: You're touring a battlefield with your family when suddenly all of you notice a ragged, tired-looking man wearing a tattered uniform walking toward you. He stops, verbalizes how thirsty he is, and asks your son if he has any water. As your son reaches for his water bottle, the man suddenly vanishes. You all stand there, flabbergasted. The fact that this ghostly apparition acknowledged your presence and attempted to communicate with your son indicates that your family just interacted with a discarnate entity.

Location represents a major factor in determining who the intelligent entities might be in these cases. It has been theorized that spirits are connected to places through strong emotional bonds. In the above example, it can be surmised that this ghost soldier either can't or won't leave the theater of war due to the traumatic circumstances surrounding his death. He appears to be bound to that location by the emotional experience of the battle, and he's at least somewhat aware of his environment because he noticed your family and even asked for some water. By rule, if a certain location is shrouded in history—meaning notable happenings took place there—the more likely it will be haunted in some way. In other words, if you discover your home was once used as a makeshift hospital during a Revolutionary War battle or was the site of a double murder/suicide, don't be surprised if spectral energies abound.

Another type of spectral event is known as a residual, or imprint, haunting, which occurs when the energy from an emotional or traumatic event "imprints" itself onto the surrounding environment. Theoretically, energy can be absorbed by rock, brick, wood, and concrete, as well as by trees, water, and the atmosphere itself. These episodes, or snippets in time, replay themselves over and over again much like a broken record or looped videotape, occurring whenever conditions become favorable or when you walk into the area of occurrence and trigger the haunting episode. Identifying these "trigger" conditions—whether atmospheric, psychic, or otherwise—remains a daunting, if not impossible, task.

Battle sites are conducive to residual hauntings. Fear, rage, despair, sorrow, and other highly charged emotions flood an environment during the course of a battle. The battle ends, but these energies linger on, providing startling and sometimes life-changing experiences to those who are present when the replay occurs. Residual hauntings can be visual, auditory, olfactory, and even gustatory in nature. The smell of sulfur, the sound of cannon fire, and even the taste of blood represent fairly common types of aberrant battlefield experiences one might have on any given day.

The major difference between a genuine haunt and a residual haunt, besides the fact that a residual haunting doesn't involve the actual spirit of a deceased person, is that during an imprint playback, the same phenomenon occurs repeatedly with no changes in the action being witnessed. For example, you're visiting Gettysburg and see a bunch of reenactors performing regimental maneuvers near the Wheatfield. They march into the Rose Woods and seem to vanish into thin air. You track down a park ranger and describe to him what happened, and he informs you no reenactors were given permits to be on the battlefield that day. He also grins as if to say, "You're not the first person to see the 'phantom regiment,'" and you walk away shaking your head. If this exemplifies a residual haunting, your description of the incident should mirror other accounts given by different witnesses, regardless of when the encounter occurred.

Another brand of high strangeness is known as an object haunting. Let's imagine you go to an antique store and buy an old locket. You bring it home, and within a week strange things start happening around your house. One of two possibilities exist in this scenario: 1. The intelligent consciousness of a deceased person, who was very attached to this locket while alive, follows you home with it. One day you see the ghostly image of an elderly woman walking down your staircase. It startles the heck out of you. Guess what? Your house is now genuinely haunted because of the presence of this locket. You bring the locket back to the antique store, and the sightings cease; or 2. The emotional energies imprinted in the locket start to affect your mood. Unbeknownst to you, the person who wore this locket in 1926 was brutally murdered. You start feeling unnaturally sad or morose whenever you wear or are near the object. You begin to experience feelings of dread and even become more prone to violence. You're now experiencing a residual energy force directly related to the locket, and you learn the hard way that you're clairvoyant. You discard the locket and start to feel better immediately.

Combat zone object hauntings are usually associated with the personal objects that belonged to soldiers who died during a battle (e.g., diaries, photos, Bibles, guns, knives, lucky charms). The presence of these objects, now buried somewhere on the field or housed in the visitor center museum, can facilitate a psi experience (a spontaneous paranormal event that occurs the moment a persons steps into an actively haunted area) and elicit strong emotional responses from visitors. The strong bonds associated with these objects can also enhance the prevalence of intelligent haunts. Let's suppose a soldier who fought at Little Round Top carried a tintype of his wife in his pocket. He was very suddenly and violently shot and killed in action. From time to time, his spirit is seen wandering around the base of Little Round Top, as if searching for something. He seems unaware of either time or his unfortunate circumstance (remember the phrases "fragment of consciousness" and "condition of emotional shock" used to define a ghost on page 12). The tintype actually was found and taken from the battlefield in 1867 by a looter, but the ghost soldier's strong connection to the photograph compels what's left of his consciousness to keep searching for it.

Although its existence is even more speculative than the more common aberrations mentioned above, portal hauntings represent another type of mysterious phenomenon that deserves mention here. Sometimes called energy vortices, portal hauntings are thought to be doorways to another world or dimension through which spirits can travel. Certain places seem to encompass a wide array of bizarre activity, including glowing balls of light, odd energy fields, strange shapes, and unexplained mists or fog. Some researchers believe these anomalies are traveling back and forth through a portal. The only evidence to support this comes in the form of high electromagnetic energy readings sometimes accompanied by a visual ripple or fluctuation in the surrounding atmosphere. The hypothetical existence of ley lines, or the alignment of a number of sacred ancient sites stretching across the planet, suggests that the Earth's natural electromagnetic energy fields often intersect at certain locations, making them prone to certain anomalies. In truth, we have experienced possible portal phenomena at Gettysburg more than once, and it appears the presence of these strong electromagnetic fields acts as a catalyst for preternatural occurrences. Timing these events, however, is difficult, and validation of the existence of these vortices isn't likely forthcoming anytime soon.

The hauntings described here represent those most commonly experienced on battlefields. Other ghostly aspects such as poltergeists, doppelgangers, shadow people, and elementals are all supported by various existential theories, but for the purposes of this book, they aren't often associated with battlefields and therefore won't be described in detail.

Attempting to quantify these experiences, regardless of their nature, represents an important, yet difficult, endeavor. If we're ever going to gain a better understanding of the human mind and spirit, we need to diligently document witness testimony and carefully measure tangible evidence in the form of electromagnetic energy spikes, ion fluctuations, temperature changes, and other anomalous readings in the environment. Capturing and documenting audio and visual phenomena in the form of photographs, video footage, and tape/digital recordings greatly enhances the possibility of turning a large body of evidence into compelling proof of the existence of ghosts. And along the way, we can honor those who came before us and, if possible, help the ghost soldiers who are stuck within their own emotional quagmire to finally move on.

We assay to document our experiences in an attempt to capture what we call "living history," or the historic moment from the perspective of the participants. In the pages that follow, you'll share in these experiences and gain a better understanding of what it may have been like to fight in the Battle of Gettysburg, where thousands of brave individuals gave the last full measure of devotion.

Chapter Two

Gettysburg's Residual Hauntings

*A*n important part of the paranormal research process is the documentation of experiencer testimony. In the world of parapsychology, "experiencer" is a fancy word for "eyewitness," or a person who has a first-hand encounter with the paranormal. During a group weekend investigation of Gettysburg, we interviewed several people who came along to learn how to conduct field investigations. As is almost always the case, many of them were there because they had experienced paranormal phenomena in the past and were hoping to learn more about what may have happened to them. One such gentleman, Brad, was fascinated with the paranormal, but particularly as it applied to battlefields. We soon learned he had experienced a life-changing encounter at Gettysburg. He provided us with the following documentation of his experience:

> In the summer of 1990 when I was seventeen years old, my parents took me on a three-week summer vacation. We drove all over the eastern half of the country, and since Civil War history was one of my passions, we spent three days in Gettysburg. I also have

a passion for ghosts and the supernatural, but I had no idea these two interests were going to come together during our visit.

Ironically, we arrived at Gettysburg on July 1 and left on July 3, the actual dates of the battle in 1863. Perhaps the timing was perfect to be able to experience the encounters I had, but whatever the reason, the following event occurred in front of my own eyes.

My encounter occurred on July 3 as we were leaving the battlefield. It was about 11 o'clock on a clear, very hot morning. As my parents and I drove through the battlefield park, I looked off to the area of a wheat field, where a particularly bloody skirmish took place during the battle. I noticed a regiment of about 30 Union soldiers marching in formation approximately 100 yards off the road, heading toward a ridge. I told my dad to stop the car; I grabbed my video camera and started sprinting across the field to catch up with them.

This Confederate sharpshooter met his violent end
in Devil's Den. Courtesy of the Library of Congress.

Many researchers believe that the manner in which these men died factors in to why the battlefield is so haunted. Courtesy of the Library of Congress.

Since we were there on the anniversary of the battle, I thought it was a reenactment group practicing some formation maneuvers. It seemed like I couldn't catch up no matter how fast I ran. I stopped on occasion and got some pretty good shots of them, but I noticed how silent they seemed to be. All you could hear was the wind rustling through the wheat. They headed over a ridge and out of site. I got to the top of the ridge about a minute later, looked around, and saw nothing for miles over an empty valley. There wasn't a single soldier in sight. There's no way they could have gone anywhere else. Beyond the ridge is a vast, open countryside, and I was less than a minute behind them.

When I got to a VCR, I popped in the tape, and sure enough, there were the soldiers as clear as day. I just knew I had videotape with ghosts on it. Every time I show it to people, they don't believe me because the soldiers are as solid as real people on video, but I know what I saw (or didn't see) when I looked over the ridge. Several years later, I saw a TV show on the ghosts of Gettysburg, and one of the stories was about visiting Japanese dignitaries who pulled their limousine over to the side of the road and watched a regiment of Union soldiers march in formation several feet in front of them. They called the park rangers and thanked them for arranging the demonstration for them, but alas, there was no demonstration arranged or scheduled.

Several other people have seen a similar phantom regiment on the battlefield, and this particular phenomenon has come to be known as the Ghost Regiment of Gettysburg. I honestly believe this is what I saw; whether people believe me or not, I know what I videotaped is the real thing.

Brad's encounter, and many other documented paranormal experiences at Gettysburg, may represent what was described in chapter 1 as residual hauntings, which theoretically occur when past events are somehow "imprinted" on environments and then experienced by eyewitnesses (via retrocognition, the ability to see past events) at a later time—sometimes decades or centuries later. The imprint theory, as you may recall, proposes that environments with traumatic emotional histories—and specifically the physical elements that make them up such as rocks, trees, water sources, man-made dwellings, etc.—act as recording devices, somehow absorbing and then replaying events that those with a sixth sense or keen intuition—or who just happen to be in the right place at the right time—can experience via visual, auditory, olfactory, and/or other sensory perceptions. Gettysburg would appear to be the perfect conduit for such activity because of its traumatic emotional history and the large scale of such trauma (51,000 + casualties in three days). Brad may have witnessed a recording of a Union regiment marching in formation 127 years prior to his visual encounter. It appears more plausible than him seeing the actual spirits of thirty separate individuals still marching in formation. This event likely constitutes an activity that occurred when these soldiers were still alive, but that was replayed more than a century later.

Loyd Auerbach, director of the Office of Paranormal Investigations and author of numerous books on the paranormal, emphasizes that residual hauntings involve the recorded activity of the living, not the dead. "Although the subject(s) of the recording may be long dead, the activity was impressed upon the environment when they were alive," he explains. "This is analogous to videotaping a person doing something—you can't really do that when the person is dead. They kind of just lie there."

Residual hauntings are most commonly referred to as "place memory" by parapsychologists and academic researchers. In less formal circles it is called "cinema of time" and is often associated with Stone Tape Theory. Andrew Nichols, PhD, professor, author, and founder of the American Institute of Parapsychology (AIP), points out that paranormal phenomena often share similar characteristics, which makes it difficult to create clear lines of distinction. For example, he says, a probable relationship exists between retrocognitive experiences and psychometry, or object reading, which is the ability to perceive information about the history and owners of an object as practiced by psychics. "In fact," he adds, "they are very likely to be very similar, if not identical, phenomenon."

Auerbach agrees that place memory seems to be an extension of psychometry. One interpretation is that the object—and what is a house but a big object—becomes a focal point for retrocognition. However, an alternative interpretation is that something about the object, building, battlefield, etc., essentially "records" information as it exists. "Human beings are capable of picking up on these environmental recordings and essentially play back bits of the information in their own perceptions/consciousness," he explains. "Most often, emotional events (or emotions themselves) are behind the more likely perceptions/recordings, although on occasion the recordings seem to be of very mundane activity."

To muddy the waters further, similar phenomena are also referred to as time slips or time warps, depending on the specific characteristics associated with them. It remains a highly debated topic within the paranormal research community, yet one that offers an incredible opportunity to learn a great deal not only about paranormal mysteries, but history itself. For example, in Brad's case, greater detail of the soldiers' uniforms may have provided researchers with an opportunity to corroborate the encounter from a historical standpoint.

Brad's Gettysburg account isn't an isolated incident, as encounters with phantom ghost armies, discarnate soldiers, and other elements from the past have been documented at length thanks to the dedication of paranormal researchers such as the late Andrew McKenzie. McKenzie, who was vice president of the Society for Psychical Research and author of many books on the paranormal, was a serious student of spontaneous cases in which protagonists found themselves in surroundings that no longer existed. His task was not a easy one. Alan Gould, a colleague of McKenzie and former professor of psychology at the University of Nottingham, professed that such cases are "fascinating, exceedingly rare, and very hard to evaluate."

One thing McKenzie learned from his research was that characteristics associated with these phenomena are similar but not always the same, which raises the question of whether a past event has been imprinted on the environment for those with psychic sensitivities to experience at a later date, or whether some type of time slip has occurred, where a person, or group of people, travel through time via supernatural means.

Two schoolteachers, Charlotte Anne Elizabeth Moberly and Eleanor Frances Jourdain, had perhaps the most famous time slip experience ever recorded. While visiting the Palace at Versailles in 1901, they decided to go in search of the Petit Trianon, a small chateau located on the grounds of the palace. While walking through the grounds, they both were impressed by a feeling of oppressive gloom. They claimed to have encountered—and interacted with—a number of people in old-fashioned attire whom they later assumed to have been members of the court of Marie Antoinette.

In a widely publicized case from 1979, two English couples driving through France claimed to have stayed overnight at an old-fashioned hotel and decided on their return journey to stay at the same hotel but were unable to find it. Photographs taken during their stay, which were in the middle of the roll of film, were missing, even from the negative strips, when the pictures were developed.

One telling characteristic of these phenomena has to do with whether those experiencing them can take an active part in the event—interacting with the people and places being "visited." In the Versailles case, the two women were apparently seen, and spoken to, by people they saw. The English couples on holiday in France went further, staying in a hotel and eating dinner and breakfast in the course of their experience. Both of these incidents represent unusually prolonged events, taking place over at least several hours. These cases are more likely associated with some sort of time slip as opposed to a residual haunting, where the subject (e.g. Brad) is merely a passive observer of the past scene—one that plays out like a movie, imprinted on paranormal celluloid.

An interesting element associated with these cases is an "altered state of reality" that's very difficult for the witnesses to describe. For example, many people report that at the start of their experiences, their immediate surroundings take on an "oddly flat, underlit, and lifeless appearance, and normal sounds seem muffled." This surreal environment is sometimes accompanied by feelings of depression and unease.

Another account includes an equally odd description of the environment, in which "the street seemed unusually quiet; there were sounds but they appeared quite muted." The witness also noticed that when she sat down, "the sun didn't seem as bright as it had been moments before." In fact, looking back years later, she described the light as similar to when the area had a partial solar eclipse.

Jenny Randles, a British author and former director of investigations with the British UFO Research Association (BUFORA), invented the phrase "Oz Factor" to describe this strange, seemingly altered state of being felt by witnesses of paranormal events. She defines the Oz Factor in her book *UFO Reality* as ... "the sensation of being isolated, or transported back from the real world into a different environmental framework ... where reality is but slightly different, as in the fairytale land of Oz."

We also experienced this Oz Factor just before hearing rebel yells in the Triangular Field at Gettysburg a few years ago (see chapter 13: "Echoes from the Past"). During that encounter, the atmosphere becoming very still and quiet just before hearing the shrieking "whoops" and "yips" that terrified Union soldiers years earlier. Oddly enough, we remembered commenting that this is what it must feel like just before one goes missing in the Bermuda Triangle.

Brad may have experienced the same phenomenon while chasing his phantom regiment at Gettysburg. Remember him describing how "I couldn't catch up no matter how fast I ran. I stopped on occasion and got some pretty good shots of them, but I noticed how silent they seemed to be. All you could hear was the wind rustling through the wheat."

One thing is certain, and that is whatever Brad saw had a profound impact on his life. He, like so many others, experienced something truly bizarre at Gettysburg. He may have been privy to a glimpse back into the past or was actually transported back in time for a few brief moments. Gettysburg most certainly acted as the catalyst for Brad's encounter due to its history and therefore most certainly requires our full attention as it applies to paranormal research and our quest to find the answers to these profound enigmas.

Chapter Three

Recordings from Another Realm

*E*lectronic voice phenomena, or EVP, represents one of the most fascinating mysteries associated with ghosts and hauntings. Basically, EVP is the reception of voice or other sound on an audiotape for which there is no known environmental source. The phenomenon is the subject of great debate within the paranormal community. Those who view the phenomenon as truly paranormal believe the recordings are either the voices of the dead trying to communicate or other residual sounds emanating from the paranormal realm. In Gettysburg, these might include cannon fire, gunshots, screams, and other sounds associated with the 1863 battle that have somehow been imprinted onto the environment and subsequently picked up on an audio recording. Skeptics, on the other hand, believe EVP recordings are nothing more than natural sounds falsely interpreted as paranormal.

Our experience with EVP tells us that both camps are correct, depending on the actual recording in question. On the one hand, many recordings capture compelling evidence of either attempted communication from the dead or residual sounds from past events. On the other hand, the human mind is the greatest puzzle solver in the known universe. Scott Flagg, a paranormal researcher and chief operating officer for the American Institute of Parapsychology, suggests that each of us must recognize our own mind's ability and desire to piece information together. As a result, simple background garble can be interpreted as actual words or specific sounds by the brain, and many recordings can be misinterpreted as paranormal in nature when in fact they aren't.

"I've personally stood around a circle of eight people listening very intently to a possible EVP recording and heard no less than eight different interpretations of what the purported voice was saying," says Flagg. His advice: avoid manipulating audio except for removing background noise, adjusting volume, and isolating elements. This will minimize the mind's opportunity to create something from nothing.

Theories abound as to how EVP might work. The Low Frequency Theory suggests that EVP occurs below the normal range of hearing (pressure waves from 0 Hz to 20 Hz) and that audio devices are somehow able to record in this range. The EMF Theory proposes that ghosts organize random electromagnetic fields to create EVP. If so, a TV set between channels or a radio tuned between stations can provide the static with which it is thought ghosts manipulate in order to "speak." A new theory suggests that very low-frequency electromagnetic fields (0 Hz to 30 Hz) can stimulate a variety of small objects, including air molecules, into motion. This process creates pressure waves that can be heard by our ears.

Regardless of how it might work, people have been interested in its applications since electronic recording devices were first invented. As early as 1928, Thomas Edison started working on equipment he hoped would permit communication with the dead. Nobody seems to know for sure how far he got with his experiments because he died before he published any results. Over time, research organizations such as the Research Association for Voice Taping and the American Association of electronic voice phenomena were founded to further our understanding of this complex enigma. One of the great pioneers of EVP research was Sarah Estep, who recorded more than 20,000 voices that she claimed were other-dimensional, extraterrestrial, or from loved ones who had passed on. She developed a classification system for EVP recordings, which is as follows:

Class A: A clear and distinct voice that can be heard without the use of headphones and can be duplicated onto other tapes.

Class B: A voice that is sometimes distinct, fairly loud, and can sometimes be heard without the use of headphones.

Class C: A faint and whispery voice that can barely be heard and is sometimes indecipherable.

Although the focus of EVP tends to be on voice communication, we should never overlook the importance of residual or imprinted sounds that often are captured on recording devices. This especially applies to a place like Gettysburg, where specific sounds are intricately connected to the environment's emotional blueprint. In fact, the frequency of EVP in the form of gunshots, cannon fire, hooves clopping, and metal clanging (military accoutrements) recorded at Gettysburg is much greater than that of communicative voices. This also applies to music, as some of the most compelling EVP I've ever heard are the sounds of music forever imprinted during the battle—"Dixie," fife and drum music, and other period melodies.

Over the years, we've collected extremely compelling EVP during our investigations at Gettysburg. In addition to the EVP mentioned above, we documented several other accounts from the battlefield. The first is from a field investigator named Coby, who was boarding with the rest of our investigative team at the Baladerry Inn Bed and Breakfast when he recorded an EVP. The Baladerry Inn is located on the actual battlefield and was used as a field hospital both during and after the battle. Bloodstains can still be seen on parts of the wooden floors.

Here is Coby's account, which was verified by team members after analysis:

In the early morning hours (approximately four a.m.) of May 7, 2004, two voices (a and b) were recorded from our room at the Baladerry Inn when we kept getting woken up for no apparent reason. Ellie took photos of the room when my K-II EMF meter started going crazy. At this time we were simply sitting up in bed talking. There are small orbs in the picture (confirmed). The voice recorder was located by the closet in the corner of the room.

a) Ellie (to Coby): We have to get that before we go … Voice (female— very matter-of-factly): How? … and then seconds later …

b) Voice (male—sighing or whispering): Okay

After analyzing the recording thoroughly, we classified this as a Class A EVP, as both voices were very clear and easy to make out. They also seemed genuine as opposed to residual, meaning some sort of communication was going on between the discarnate voices and the people staying in the room. This cannot be verified of course, but it constitutes very compelling EVP evidence.

The second account occurred during the same weekend investigation. While investigating at Spangler's Spring on the evening of May 7, 2004, we coordinated various team members to establish secluded areas in which to conduct EVP experiments. We asked a particular field investigator named Heather to take her microcassette recorder and sit on a rock by the actual spring. Once there, she performed an EVP experiment during which she asked certain questions in twenty-second intervals, thus providing enough time for a possible response. Upon playback of her tape, she ran to us in a rather excited state and suggested she may have captured something. When we listened to the recording, we all heard the following very clearly at the midpoint of her questioning:

Heather: Do you like it here?

Voice (male—low but clearly audible): Hell no!

Once again, we classified this as a Class A EVP. The voice was male, and you could hear the words *"Hell no!"* very distinctly on the tape. It was most likely a genuine contact, as a form of conscious energy was clearly responding to her question. Unfortunately, in regards to Heather's recording, the voice she captured mysteriously disappeared after a couple of weeks. At first we thought she must have accidentally erased it, but she was adamant about being careful with it. Plus, EVP mysteriously disappearing from magnetic tape is *not* unheard of. There are many instances of this happening, as if the sound was only audible for a short period of time.

EVP is a promising, yet frustrating, area of study within the world of paranormal research. There are only so many ways one can analyze EVP recordings. You can utilize sound programs to clean them up (eliminate background noise, etc.), and you can use computer programs to analyze sound waves and determine at what frequency these sounds are emanating. But as of now we have no way to determine if these recordings are from another realm or simply the result of our minds making sense of chaos.

Chapter Four

Photos from Another Realm

*O*ver the years, we've been fortunate enough to capture a wide variety of paranormal photographs at Gettysburg. Before these "spirit" photos can be analyzed accurately, however, it's important to understand the nature of photography, the history and nature of paranormal photographs, and how to distinguish between genuine paranormal captures and camera glitches, light anomalies, or user errors.

One of the most important inventions in history, photography has transformed the way people see the world. With the click of a button, we can capture moments in time and preserve them for years to come. Every so often—at least in theory—we can capture images not seen with the naked eye . . . images that suggest the existence of paranormal phenomena and defy our understanding of the physical world.

Currently, two technologies make creating photographs possible: traditional film technology and digital imaging technology. Traditional film technology, which dates back almost two hundred years, exposes a visual image onto special light-sensitive chemicals within the film. The film contains a physical representation of the image and, once exposed, the transparencies and negatives last for decades. A much newer technology, digital imaging creates a digital representation according to the color and intensity of light falling on an array of special digital receptors. A specialized form of microchip, these sensors measure the amount of light that falls on different parts of the sensor surface in a given time window. The images are digital files stored in digital memory.

People have been capturing ghostly images on film since the early days of photography. Unfortunately, many of the first spirit photos taken in the mid-to-late 1800s were hoaxes, cleverly created by psychic mediums professing to be communicating directly with the dead. Obvious frauds, these photos showed individuals sitting in chairs with the faces of their deceased loved ones hovering in the air around them. Some were even more dubious, showing mediums in supposed trance states spewing ectoplasm (a gauze-like substance associated with the formation of spirits) out of their mouths as they connected with the spirit world.

However, much more compelling photographs—such as the Combermere Abbey ghost taken in 1891, the Brown Lady of Raynham Hall taken in 1936, and the Tulip Staircase ghost taken in 1966—clearly defy conventional thinking and demand further inquiry. Over the years, thousands of honest and credible people from all walks of life have taken compelling pictures that show various types of paranormal anomalies, including spirit mists and orbs, energy vortexes, and more evidentially convincing apparitional forms, which often show clearly defined facial and body features.

So, can ghostly activity—invisible to the naked eye—be captured on film? Assuming ghosts exist, certain facts regarding human vision and camera mechanics suggest that the answer to this question is "yes." First, let's consider the visible light spectrum. Our eyes are sensitive to light that lies in a very small region of the electromagnetic spectrum known as visible light (which corresponds to a wavelength range of 400 to 700 nanometers and a color range of violet through red). The human eye isn't capable of seeing radiation within wavelengths outside the visible spectrum. For example, ultraviolet radiation has a shorter wavelength than visible violet light, and infrared radiation has a longer wavelength than visible red light. In traditional film technology, photographic emulsions are more sensitive and can capture wavelengths beyond the visible spectrum. Digital sensors are also sensitive to a range of light wider than we can see. The full, broad spectrum of a film or camera sensor bandwidth can be enhanced even further with the help of various filters and film types. Some researchers theorize that energy patterns of ghosts fall into a spectrum of light that isn't visible to the human eye. If so, it might be possible to capture undetected spirit energy that manifests outside visible wavelengths with either a digital or film camera.

Shutter speed is another variable that may account for the existence of paranormal photographs. Vision is a continuous process of the human eye, but eyelids act as shutters that create a small time gap between two continuous visions. This small time gap is the shutter speed that is adjustable in a camera but natural in the eye. On average, an eye has a shutter speed of around 1/50 of a second. The shutter speed of a camera can be as fast as 1/4000 of a second. If someone fired a gun and the bullet whizzed by, you wouldn't be able to see it, but a camera set at a fast shutter speed could freeze its movement.

The possible nature of spirit might also explain this enigma. Some religious scholars and spiritual practitioners have theorized that spirit energy exists on a higher—and faster—metaphysical plane than humans (who exist on a slower, material plane). If such energy vibrates at an accelerated rate, it might explain why people see shadows or figures moving "out of the corner of their eyes." Theoretically, these fast-moving energy forms can be photographed with the faster shutter speeds associated with camera mechanics.

Another theory suggests that ghosts only make themselves visible when they want to and that paranormal photographs are "gifts" from the beyond. This may be true, as some researchers believe ghosts absorb energy from their surrounding environments in order to create physical anomalies, including manifesting in the presence of certain individuals. Based on this theory, you could conceivably ask permission of the spirits to allow you to photograph them and hope for the best. Many field investigators have employed this method in an attempt to communicate with these entities.

Over the years, we've captured all types of visual anomalies thanks to the diligent efforts of both our field research team and our weekend investigation guests. The following accounts all have powerful photographic evidence to go along with the eyewitness testimony.

Little Round Top Face

During the second day of fighting, when Confederate soldiers advanced against the Union army's left flank positioned on Little Round Top, they had to maneuver through the boulders of Devil's Den and across a little stream known as Bloody Run. Members of the Texas and Alabama regiments who managed to make it this far found themselves in a wooded area at the southern base of Little Round Top. It was here where they regrouped and began their uphill assaults against Union Col. Joshua Chamberlain's Twentieth Maine.

While investigating this area a few years ago, one of the psychics in our group picked up on the presence of a soldier at the base of the hill. We immediately took some EMF readings and registered slightly elevated electromagnetic energy levels. Other team members took photographs of and around the psychic to try and capture any spirit energy that may have been manifesting around her. After about ten minutes, the readings dissipated and the psychic informed us that the presence was no longer there.

Later that evening, while downloading digital camera files, we noticed an anomaly in one of the photos that was taken at the base of Little Round Top. We zoomed in on the object in question, and we clearly saw a man's face. Sporting a mustache and hat, he had clearly defined features and genuinely looked like a Civil War soldier. Compelled by the details, we tried to figure out what else it could be by process of elimination. After ruling out glares and other camera glitches, we were left with two possibilities. It was either a genuine paranormal capture or a case of simulacra (an unreal or vague semblance of something).

Supporting the genuine paranormal capture assumption is the fact that the psychic sensitive was picking up on the presence of a soldier at the time the photo was taken, and we also documented elevated electromagnetic energy levels in the area. Simulacra, on the other hand, can be likened to a case of mistaken identity, which occurs because our minds naturally tend to create order out of chaos. In a scenario where trees, bushes, rocks, and leaves fill a photograph's frame, people tend to interpret what they see based on what they are more familiar with, such as an animal or a person's face. In reality, the mind is simply trying to put the pieces of a chaotic puzzle together as not to cause confusion.

In this particular case, the anomaly stands out clearly. One doesn't have to struggle to create this face in the bushes because it's literally staring right back at you. Another factor that weakens the case for simulacra relates to the corroborative nature of the image and where it was taken. For example, if we had suggested a white tiger was in the photograph, it wouldn't make sense geographically. White tigers are indigenous to Southeast Asia, so why would a ghost of one of these magnificent creatures be captured in Gettysburg unless an old zoo once stood on that spot (which isn't the case). Instead, we clearly see a man's face—complete with mustache and hat—which resembles the prototypical individual who might have died at the base of Little Round Top—a Civil War soldier! Does this confirm a genuine paranormal capture? We can never be completely sure of that, but this photograph definitely represents one of the most persuasive we've ever captured.

Devil's Den Apparition

During one of our visits to the battlefield, we were walking among the rocks in Devil's Den when Jack felt the urge to meander into the wooded area to the south of where the heavy fighting took place. He walked down a small pathway about two hundred yards from the big boulders where he felt a profound sense of quiet and stillness. His intuition told him to take photographs of the surrounding area. Nothing of particular interest stuck out in this thicket of trees, yet he felt the need to shoot around fifteen frames of film with his still camera (no flash). He stayed there for about twenty minutes and then caught up with the rest of the group, who were making their way over to the Triangular Field.

When Jack developed the film, he noticed something strange in one of the photos. He knew immediately that it didn't belong there, and when he looked closer, he saw a white figure walking among the trees. Startled, he produced a close-up of the image and knew he had captured something interesting—a figure of a person walking with some type of satchel or small suitcase in one hand. This "individual" also appeared to be wearing a hat and a dress, which made me surmise that it was a woman. The analytical process kicked in as he tried to make sense of the photograph. How did he photograph a female form walking behind Devil's Den? Why is she, or he, carrying a bag? And the obvious question: Why did he capture something that he didn't see with his naked eye?

One of the fun things about ghost hunting is that you get to immerse yourself in history. In fact, the historical context of what you might be experiencing can shed a great deal of light on the phenomenon itself. Nothing (that we know of) happens in a complete vacuum. The philosophical concept of cause and effect still seems to dictate the "who, what, when, where, and why" of paranormal activity. By thoroughly studying the history of a haunted location, you can create an accurate road map that can guide you through your investigation and give you a better idea of what you're dealing with.

With this photograph, Jack knew he needed more information in order to make a better assessment of it. He researched why women might be on the Gettysburg battlefield and was thoroughly enlightened. At night, when the fighting usually subsided, nurses and doctors searched the terrain for wounded soldiers in need of assistance. They usually did this with a lantern and a bag full of medicines they needed to ease the soldiers' suffering. At Gettysburg, the carnage was so great that wounded men often lay where they fell for days before receiving any help. After the battle was over and the remnants of the two armies left, the townspeople and a small group of doctors and nurses were faced with what must have been a daunting and emotionally draining task—taking care of the dead and wounded.

We now had a reference point from which to objectively quantify the photograph. Women did indeed walk on this battlefield in July 1863, and they would most certainly have been overwhelmed with strong, intense emotions as they performed their grisly tasks as caregivers among some of the greatest carnage ever manifested on American soil.

We also realized that the nature of a haunting can sometimes be more mundane. Gettysburg represents more than just a three-day battle that took place almost 150 years ago. Many generations of individuals lived and died in this area over the course of time without having been privy to the horrors of war. Native Americans also inhabited the area for hundreds of years before Europeans began to settle on the continent. Therefore, from a logical standpoint, the apparitional form in the photograph could be anyone from any number of time periods. However, considering the history of this specific location and the details in the photo, it seems more likely that this could be an energy imprint from the actual battle (or its aftermath).

Baladerry Inn Soldiers

The Gettysburg battlefield is dotted with farmhouses, some of which were standing during the time of the battle. In just about every case, these homes were used as either field hospitals to accommodate the overwhelming amount of wounded men or as headquarters for the highest-ranking officers. Located behind Little Round Top on the eastern edge of the battlefield, the Baladerry Inn was no exception. Now a bed and breakfast, it stood witness to the horrors of July 1863 and still bears the bloodstains on its dining room floor to prove it.

Over the years, we've enjoyed great accommodations and warm hospitality at the Baladerry, whose guests have had their fair share of ghostly encounters. We learned from the proprietor that people often see soldiers peering through the windows as if they are curious about what's happening inside. Witnesses have also reported seeing a particularly mischievous soldier who enjoys playfully annoying female patrons. Once, during a meeting we held in the living room, we heard a loud popping sound directly above the head of a young female investigator. Her digital recorder ceased to function, and she became hot and exasperated, as if something, or someone, was purposely encroaching on her personal space.

Late one evening, we were reviewing evidence in the living room while one of our weekend investigation participants took random photographs in the house. After taking a picture from the staircase looking out onto the back deck, she suddenly gasped and said, "Guys, you need to come look at this." We immediately walked over and crowded around her digital camera.

"See outside the French doors, by the lattice?" she asked.

At first, we didn't notice anything because we were looking in the wrong area, but we eventually focused on the right spot and let out a gasp of our own.

"You've got to be kidding me," said Jack.

Standing outside by the deck were two men dressed in uniforms, looking directly into the living room. They seemed semitransparent, but we could clearly make out the shapes of their bodies, including heads, necks, torsos and arms. They also appeared to be wearing hats.

"Is anyone outside?" asked Jack.

We were pretty sure everyone had already gone to bed, but we needed to confirm this. We cautiously ventured out the patio doors and thoroughly checked the entire property, but we found nothing. After downloading the picture onto a computer, we approximated where the figures had been standing when the picture was taken. The next day, we compared the angle of the photo to the deck area and determined that the figures would have been standing in a row of large, thick bushes. This was a problem for several reasons. First, two people couldn't have been standing in that row of bushes because there was absolutely no room to do so. Additionally, the deck was raised, so if the men had actually been standing there, they would have been at least eight feet tall! As with most paranormal photographs, we were left scratching our heads.

Two interesting factors make this photograph worthy of serious discussion. According to the owner of the property, dozens of individuals have reported seeing soldiers looking through the windows, gazing into the house. As such, this represents supportive evidence. Also, their presence fits the property's historic profile. We didn't capture two people wearing Polo shirts and shorts; we photographed two men wearing what look like uniforms. During the battle, hundreds of soldiers wandered around this property, either because they were wounded, lost, or looking for fallen comrades. It is at least plausible, therefore, that we may have photographed the spirits of two of them.

Triangular Field Soldiers

Capturing an apparition in a photograph is rare; capturing three of them—all dressed in Army of the Potomac uniforms—simply strains credulity. We discuss the Triangular Field a great deal in this book for good reason. With so much paranormal activity reported on and around this small patch of land, we tend to spend a great deal of time there performing all manner of experiments.

We love twilight on the battlefield. Also known as "the gloaming," this is the period after sunset but before dark when the environment seems surreal. As our eyes adjust to the coming darkness, our surroundings feel different, as if we are teetering on the edge of two separate realities. And so it was on this day, as we attempted to capture some of the anomalies so often described in the Triangular Field.

During this particular investigation, we were fortunate to have a well-reputed psychic medium with us. At dusk, the area was devoid of people, so we thought it might be a good time to follow her into the field and document her reactions. With Jack's camera at his side, he instructed her to start at the fence and walk slowly down to the bottom of the field. Halfway down, she stopped in her tracks and told us to take pictures of the area below her by the tree line. As she continued to walk, she picked up on the presence of both Union and Confederate soldiers.

"The air is very heavy here," she observed. "There are men just wandering all around us. It's like nothing I've ever experienced before."

Happy with the results, we finished the experiment and returned to the Baladerry Inn (aka our base camp), where we began to analyze our video and sound recordings, as well as our photographs. This process is often tedious and unrewarding, but on this night, we were in for a big surprise.

"Were there any reenactors on the field tonight?" asked a team member.

"No, the field was empty. Nobody was there," Jack responded.

"Well, if that's true, you better come look at this," she said.

What we proceeded to look at was nothing short of astonishing. Beyond the forward glance of the psychic, down by the tree line to her right, were two figures wearing light blue pants and dark blue jackets. They seemed to be either walking or running. To the left of the psychic, we noticed another man down by the edge of the woods. Sitting on a rock or tree stump, he was wearing light blue pants and a dark blue jacket, as well as a dark blue kepi. We hadn't seen these men in the field, and there's no way we could've missed them, so where did they come from?

Capturing the spirit forms of three Union soldiers in one photograph seems most implausible ... yet there they were, doing whatever soldiers do when wandering around the place where they probably met their demise. Did the camera catch a glimpse of the actual battle, which manifested at that particular moment due to residual energies still present—yet not visible to the naked eye—on the field of battle?

It's very difficult to verify anomalous photographs as proof of the existence of ghostly phenomena—whether genuine, residual, or otherwise. On the other hand, we can't simply dismiss all of these photographs as camera glitches or user error because they often show clear, identifiable images that corroborate unexplained activity that occurred in those specific locations. In the examples above, we feel these images represent strong evidence in favor of the presence of either spirit or residual energies. We'll probably never know for sure if these pictures have revealed a glimpse into the spiritual realm, but we owe it to ourselves to consider all possibilities.

Day One

July 1, 1863

On July 1, 1863, the lead elements of Confederate Gen. Robert E. Lee's Army of Northern Virginia moved toward Gettysburg in the belief that much-needed shoes for rebel soldiers (who often marched barefoot) were being protected by local militia. Confederate Gen. Henry Heth of Gen. A. P. Hill's Third Corps soon found out that instead of militia, he faced the seasoned veterans of Gen. John Buford's First Division of the Union Cavalry of the Army of the Potomac. Buford engaged Heth at Herr's Ridge and applied a tactic called depth-in-defense, in which a smaller force engages a larger number of troops and fights them long enough to slow their advance, then falls back and deploys in a new line of defense. Buford's goal was to slow the Confederate advance until Union infantry could arrive and engage the enemy on equal terms.

Buford held off the Confederate advance long enough for Union infantry to arrive, with Gen. John Reynolds First Corps positioning on McPherson Ridge and Gen. Oliver Howard's Eleventh Corps defending the area just north of Gettysburg. The initial Confederate assaults down the Chambersburg Pike were repulsed, but at great cost to the Union First Corps, as General Reynolds became the first general killed at the Battle of Gettysburg. The Confederate Second Corps, under Gen. Richard Ewell, then began a massive assault from the north, with Gen. Robert Rodes's division attacking from Oak Hill and Gen. Jubal Early's division attacking across the open fields north of town, crashing into Howard's Eleventh Corps, crushing the left flank of the Union line. At the same time, Confederate Gen. Dorsey Pender's Division struck the First Corps, who had fallen back to Seminary Ridge. Their attack was so ferocious that the weary men of the First Corps began to give ground, and when the Eleventh Corps line collapsed around four p.m., the entire Army of the Potomac was retreating through the town of Gettysburg. They took up good defensive positions on Cemetery Hill and waited for additional attacks. Despite discretionary orders from General Lee to take the heights "if practicable," General Ewell chose not to attack. Historians have debated ever since how the battle might have ended differently if he had found it practicable to do so.

Just over 9,000 Union soldiers were casualties on the first day's action; of those, slightly more than 3,000 were taken prisoner. For the Confederates, total casualties reached 6,500. To put this into perspective, in 12 hours of fighting, there was a combined causality rate of 1,292 soldiers per hour, which means that for every minute of fighting, 22 men were killed, wounded, or captured.

Seminary Ridge

ELLIOTT'S
MAP OF THE
BATTLEFIELD OF GETTYSBURG
PENNSYLVANIA

Chapter Five

High Strangeness on
Seminary Ridge

— By Jack Roth —

On May 8, 2004, we decided to set up a private midnight tour of Seminary Ridge for the investigative team and our guests. We had heard of many ghostly encounters in this area and, we knew it would be very quiet and free of tourists at such a late hour.

Seminary Ridge was the site of fierce fighting on the first day of the battle. This was where Union Gen. John Buford's Cavalry Corps First Division held off Gen. Henry Heth's superior Confederate infantry forces long enough for corps of Union infantry to arrive at Gettysburg. The beautiful Lutheran Theological Seminary dominates the geography of Seminary Ridge, as it sits majestically on its crest. It was to its highest cupola where Buford, while trying to lead his troops from the field, climbed up periodically to assess a broader view of a very grave situation—pivoting constantly with binoculars to watch both his badly outnumbered cavalry division holding off the Confederates to the north and for any sign of Union General Reynolds's I Corps arriving from either the south or west.

Union General John Buford, whose Cavalry Corps First Division held off superior Confederate Infantry until Union infantry could arrive at Gettysburg on July 1, 1863. Courtesy of the Library of Congress.

Union dead next to McPherson's Woods after the first
day of fighting. Courtesy of the Library of Congress.

Our tour began peacefully enough, as our knowledgeable guide gave us a detailed description of both the Lutheran Seminary and the riveting events of the battle's first day. But then, as is often the case in Gettysburg, what had been an uneventful midnight stroll slowly transformed into an emotional whirlwind of high strangeness. After the tour ended and the excitement subsided, we decided to get everyone back to our hotel in order to lead a roundtable discussion while the night's "festivities" were still fresh in everyone's memories.

One of our guests, Shannon, was the first to describe what she saw. Apparently, as she was listening to the tour guide, she saw a pinpoint of light streak over the top of her head. The light wasn't visible for very long and quickly disappeared. She described it as moving from left to right over the tour guide's head.

"Can you describe the light?" I asked.

"It was more of a small pinpoint streaking across the sky," replied Shannon. "Not even an inch, which is why I thought it was a bug at first."

Sean, another tour participant, also witnessed something similar. "I think I saw the same thing at a different time," he said. "I didn't really think much about it. It was when she was talking about the widow's house, and I saw it seven to ten feet above her head, starting off at golf-ball size and trailing about six feet. It was yellow and reddish. It got no bigger than a softball."

I asked if anyone else saw something.

"Debbie, when you were looking through the window at the Seminary, I walked over and I took a picture of the steps, and then I saw that you were looking in the window," said Sean. "So I decided to take a picture of you, and just as I lifted my camera I saw a light about ten or twelve feet away on my right-hand side on the ground. And it wasn't the blue orbs that I've seen in your photos. This was something I've never seen in digital camera displays, but it was a light on the ground and then it was just gone. Something was definitely there and then it wasn't there; and it wasn't somebody else taking a picture because everybody else was standing at another location."

"Could it have been a flashlight?" I asked.

"No," Sean said. "Nobody else was there. It was totally dark on that side of the steps and I didn't know she was there. I don't know why I walked over there. This is the first time I've done anything like this."

I added that when the tour guide was talking about John Reynolds, I was looking around the street corner where some houses were, in the same direction she said they took General Reynolds's body. I looked over and saw this white figure moving toward the street corner. There was a big bush on the corner, so I saw this glowing form for about two or three seconds, and it was higher up ... it was probably about five or six feet off the ground. It happened really quickly, so I thought it might be a person walking with a bright white shirt. At least that's what I assumed at first, and then I waited for it to turn the corner and come out from the other side of the bush that was blocking my view, but it never did. I kept staring at the same location and wanted to make sure nothing came out the other side, and nothing ever did. If a person was walking down the street, they would have eventually come out from the other side of the bush because that's where the street went."

Jon added to the list of phenomena we experienced that night. "When we first arrived for the ghost tour, I was standing to the side looking at something on Seminary Ridge, and it looked like a cat," he described. "It was oblong and black, maybe the size of a football. And it kind of bounded down the hill a little bit. There was this bushy shrub tree, and it went behind that and disappeared. I poked Jack and we walked down there to make sure it wasn't a cat or something in the tree. We actually walked down past the tree, and there was nothing in the tree. There was nowhere for it to jump out, and I watched the tree the entire time."

(left) A ghostly mist forms in McPherson's Woods, where heavy fighting took place on the first day of the battle. (right) Second still from video shows mist forming and moving like someone running with what looks like a gun. Photos by Michael Hartness.

Robin, who had been with us on a few Gettysburg investigations in the past and was a very reliable witness, said that she was standing by the church steeple toward the end of the tour, and she had this feeling in her peripheral vision as if something was going to happen to her right. "So I turned around, took a few steps away from the tour guide, and thought I saw what appeared to be soldiers," she said. "It was just a couple of them at first moving between the trees. This is when Debbie (a sensitive) came over, probably out of concern. There was such a strong odor of gunpowder that my eyes started tearing. And it was so bitterly cold that my camera froze. The batteries did not fail; the camera froze. The zoom lens wouldn't move, and nothing would work. Debbie came over, which was comforting because when you're in the midst of something like that away from the group, you want somebody around."

Debbie jumped in with her perspective. "I walked over to her because she was standing perfectly still, so I thought something was going on," she said. "As soon as I started walking toward her, the closer I got to her, the colder it got. By the time I got in front of her, I could smell the gunpowder, and we're both sniffing the air and asking, 'Well, what do you smell?' She's telling me she's smelling gunpowder, and I'm smelling the same thing, so I knew we weren't both hallucinating this strange odor, and it was freezing cold."

"It was freezing!" added Robin.

"I mean it was cold to begin with, but this was a bone-chilling cold," continued Debbie. "This went right through your skin like a deep, frigid cold. And then we lost you guys for a bit and had to find you again, and as the tour guide was telling the story about the soldier who was accidentally buried alive, we were looking again at that same area because the other thing we had seen was two columns of white, kind of misty, floating material. And we both saw it."

"Just coming up from the earth," said Robin. "A mist."

"But it didn't belong there; it wasn't supposed to be there and it wasn't right . . . there was no mist anyplace else," said Debbie. "So then we were walking toward it, and the closer we got to that little grove of trees, the colder it was getting. We stopped and just watched. And you could see deeper shadows, but they were definitely people-shaped shadows moving between the trees, and they were definitely moving.

"Robin, how many were there?" I asked.

"There was a group of three, and there was another pair of two, and there was another group of at least four," she said. "We were really careful to point out where and in what direction they were moving. Whether it was at the streetlight, to the right of the streetlight, or ahead of the tree. We were really careful to identify movement to each other to make sure we weren't seeing car taillights or something like that."

"A lot of mysterious shadows and lights," I said. "Anything else?"

"When we left, we got turned around on Seminary Ridge and wound up on Confederate Avenue, so we got to ride along where Pickett's division formed before Pickett's Charge and all the way down to the end of the Confederate line," said Jon. "I mean, it's miles and miles of tree line and monuments and cannons and everything else, and as we drove down, I saw a large rectangular light, a bright light out in the middle of the battlefield. It was distinctly purple and as large as one of the monuments. It was as if somebody put a purple film in front of a light to make the light change color. It was bright and purple, and it was basically lit up in the middle of the battlefield."

I pointed out to everyone that I was in the car with Jon and Scott, and both of their reactions were interesting because they reacted at exactly the same time to whatever they saw.

"Yeah, I saw it too," said Scott. "It was the weirdest thing. We tried to come up with a rational explanation of what it could have been, but we couldn't. It was one of the weirdest things I've ever seen. And why purple? It's been a very strange night."

After the roundtable discussion, Scott and Jon stayed up a while longer to tell me about their interpretation of the streaking light they also saw on Seminary Ridge. I didn't know they had also seen a similar phenomenon, so I was interested to hear what they had to say.

"We were standing out there just enjoying the tour," Scott began. "The tour guide had set down her lantern, and we were all gathered around in a semicircle. Suddenly, almost thirty feet above us, I saw a very intense, extremely bright white streak of light. It wasn't a ball of light casting a contrail; it wasn't any fixed thing. It was just like a stretch of light that was about three to four feet long. It started out about three or four inches wide and as it went along, it stretched and elongated a little bit, and then it just dissipated. It kind of looked like a glowing surfboard, to be honest with you. So basically, it started about twenty-five feet above us, and it went and kind of streaked away."

"I think I saw the other end of what Scott saw," Jon continued. "When I first got to that spot, instead of listening to the tour I was watching the top of the Seminary to try and see if I could see anything up in the tower. I saw shadows up there move like somebody hit it with a flashlight, and I looked around to tell somebody but I didn't see anybody else looking that way, so I was going to wait until the end of the tour, but that's when I heard the others talking about seeing a light coming from one way and then dissipate going the other way. But that's what I saw. The tour guide also told us she saw the same thing happen about two or three times before we got there. Her husband saw it once and she saw it twice—a light from that general area streaking across the sky, but it never followed the same pattern twice. And there were no lighthouses or searchlights around there, so it couldn't have been that."

"And what you saw was moving in the same trajectory as what I saw," added Scott. "But what I saw faded out, so it's almost like Jon was looking in a different direction, and whatever it was kind of re-intensified later on down the line but at the same trajectory."

These eyewitness accounts illustrate just how hard it is to accurately describe and define paranormal incidents. Each person who saw the streaking light on Seminary Ridge most likely saw the same thing but had a different interpretation of what it looked like. In this case, one person's bug was another person's ghostly surfboard.

Different interpretations aside, notice how in a group setting as one person starts to open up about experiencing something, other people start to feel more comfortable about it and chime in with their own experiences. It started with a flash of light in the sky that Shannon thought might be a bug, but thankfully she wasn't afraid to mention it. From that we obtained compelling and corroborative testimony involving other strange lights, moving shadows, glowing figures, the overwhelming smell of gunpowder, shadowy soldier figures, and a huge flash of purple light seen right where Pickett's men would have congregated to prepare for their famous charge. This is why having roundtable discussions (in a relaxed atmosphere) after a paranormal event is an effective way to draw out and document eyewitness testimony.

That night on Seminary Ridge was one of the most interesting nights I've ever spent in Gettysburg, but what exactly did we see? Surprisingly, seeing flashes and streaks of light on the battlefield is more common than one might think. Some theorize these may represent the imprinted energies of both gun and cannon fire, which is certainly a plausible explanation considering the concentrated amount that was expelled in a three-day period. As for smelling the gunpowder, this too could easily represent a residual haunting, as the entire battlefield and surrounding countryside must have been permeated with the smell of gunpowder (and other, much more ghastly things) for days. Regarding the shadows and the glowing figures, we'll probably never know; we obtained no photographic evidence to corroborate the visual sightings.

In the end, these experiences left us with more questions than answers, but by documenting them, we may someday be able to develop a viable blueprint as to the nature of paranormal activity. And perhaps more importantly, engaging in the pursuit of these answers allows us to witness profound events and learn a great deal about—if nothing else—the human experience.

Chapter Six

The Mississippi
Boys Join In

— By Patrick Burke —

*I*t was late in September 2004 when my team was asked to take a group
of investigators to Gettysburg. They wanted to see some hot spots
where we had experienced paranormal phenomena on previous investigations. I took a small group to the Copse of Trees on Cemetery Ridge, just
behind the stone wall where Confederate Gen. Lewis Armistead crossed over
during Trimble/Pickett's Charge. After I was done with this guided walkthrough, I decided to visit the site of the William Bliss Farmhouse and Barn,
which stood in the no-man's land between the Confederate forces on Seminary Ridge and the Union army on Cemetery Ridge. On the evening after
the first day's battle, Union sharpshooters moved into the Bliss Farm House
and Barn. The next morning, General Posey's Mississippi troops were sent
to drive the Yankees out. This resulted in the Bliss Farm being the subject of
fierce fighting on both the second and third days of the battle and was the
perfect place for sharpshooters on both sides to harass their enemy. It was
also the site of a great controversy.

*Union Commanding General George Meade's headquarters was on
Cemetery Ridge, where Confederate forces focused the brunt of their
attack on the third day of the battle. Courtesy of the Library of Congress.*

I wanted to get a head start, so I told the group I would meet them
at the Bliss Farm. At approximately nine p.m., I began my short drive to
Seminary Ridge. The night was cool and I could see my breath in the chilly
air. A scattering of clouds danced with the moon. I pulled over to the side of
the road near where Confederate Gen. Carnot Posey's Mississippi Brigade
started their attack on July 2, 1863. I turned off the car lights and stepped
into the pitch black of night. I stood there for several minutes acclimating

to the night sounds and let my eyes adjust to the darkness. I felt as if I was being watched, which is something I've experienced many times before during battlefield investigations. I quietly said "hello" and poured some water for any thirsty souls who might be present.

I crossed the road toward the open fields of the Bliss Farm and wondered what it must have been like for Posey and his men during the battle. Posey's brigade was composed of four Mississippi regiments of infantry, and formed part of Gen. Richard Anderson's division of Gen. A. P. Hill's Third Corps. The brigade assisted in the attack against the Union positions along Cemetery Ridge and toward the heights of Little Round Top and the Devil's Den on July 2.

On that day, a Union skirmish line held the Bliss Farmhouse and Barn, but Posey's brigade attacked and took hold of the buildings for a short time until Union reinforcements forced them to retreat. The Mississippians re-formed and drove the Union troopers out of the farmhouse and barn, but instead of advancing and supporting Gen. Ambrose Wright's Georgia Brigade on their right, they stayed and held the buildings. The controversy as to whether Posey had orders to hold his position or advance to Cemetery Ridge and help Wright remains unsettled today.

In *The War of the Rebellion: A Compilation of the Official Records of the Union and Confederate Armies*, Wright reported:

> We were now within less than 100 yards of the crest of the heights, which were lined with artillery, supported by a strong line of infantry, under protection from a stone fence. My men, by a well-directed fire, soon drove the cannoneers from their guns, and, leaping over the fence, charged up the top of the crest, and drove the enemy's infantry into a rocky gorge on the eastern slope of the heights, and some 80 or 100 yards in rear of the enemy's batteries. We were now complete masters of the field, having gained the key, as it were, of the enemy's whole line.

Wright could have maintained the heights on Cemetery Ridge, changing the complexity of the battle dramatically, but through some strange twist of fate he wasn't supported in his advance. He continued in his report:

> Unfortunately, just as we had carried the enemy's last and strongest position, it was discovered that the brigade on our right had not only not advanced across the turnpike, but had actually given way and was rapidly falling back to the rear, while on our left we were entirely unprotected, the brigade ordered to our support having failed to advance ... I have not the slightest doubt but that I should have been able to have maintained my position on the heights, and secured the captured artillery, if there had been a protecting force on my left, or if the brigade on my right had not been forced to retire.

Perception is relative. From Wright's point of view, he was let down by Posey and other Confederate forces, but what about Posey's perception of the facts? If he did, in fact, receive orders to hold the Bliss Farm, he would have obeyed those orders and felt an immense amount of pride in doing so. Although Posey did send several regiments forward at different times, he never advanced in force, which was the original concept and plan that Lee put forth. Two of Posey's regiments, the Nineteenth and Forty-Eighth Mississippi, did advance forward with Wright's brigade all the way to Brian's Barn near Ziegler's Grove, but they were told by an officer to fall back, not once, but three times.

Unfortunately, conflicting recollections and the passage of time have clouded what happened on that day. Some historians, and the people who read specific accounts like Wright's above, will always believe that Posey's brigade somehow failed in their duty, which isn't fair to the brave Mississippians who fought so hard to secure this strategic patch of land.

After I offered up some water to the thirsty troops, I stepped over the rock wall and into the open field toward the Bliss Farm. Suddenly, the feeling of extreme hunger struck me. "Odd," I thought to myself. "I just ate a satisfying meal at the Lincoln Diner." Could I be having an interactive experience with one of Posey's men? I knew that the troops had not had a hot meal that day.

I entered the field just as the moon broke through some clouds and bathed the field in front of me in moonlight. "Well boys," I said aloud in a Southern drawl, "I'll be stepping off now to the farm ahead; you can join me if you've a mind to." As soon as I started walking, a rush of energy hit me violently—apprehension, anticipation, fear, and determination all mingled together in a tidal wave of emotion.

This makes a person wonder how they might react in a battlefield situation. I began to pick up my pace, feeling the need to gain the cover of the farmhouse as quickly as possible. Off to my right, I heard several men walking; seconds later, the same sounds came from my left. Was this a residual haunting or a genuine, live interaction? Ghosts react to our energy, and there are many times when we walk into a room or area and set off a genuine haunting experience. It was almost 800 yards to the remains of the Bliss farmhouse and another 200 yards to where the barn used to be. The ghost soldiers continued to walk with me until I saw the LED flashlight of one of my team members pointed in my direction. Before I headed back toward the group, I stopped and said thank you to the Mississippi boys for their company, and bid them farewell.

I can only wonder if some of the fallen soldiers from Posey's brigade still walk the fields in and around the Bliss Farm area, waiting to be vindicated from any controversies related to their actions on July 2, 1863, when the chaos and confusion of battle often prevailed over objective thinking.

Spangler's Spring

Chapter Seven

Gut Shot Soldier

— By Patrick Burke —

Sometimes you capture the most incredible paranormal evidence when you least expect it. As a case in point, a few years ago I was trying out my new infrared camcorder and wanted to see how it would record when shooting at dusk in the near-infrared format. I decided to film at Spangler's Spring, partly because I'd never filmed there before and partly because of the time of day, around seven thirty p.m. The sun was setting behind the trees near the spring, which would help eliminate any direct sunlight that might cause the image to become completely overexposed as a result of too much light pouring into the lens aperture.

A natural spring that flows at the southern end of Culp's Hill, Spangler's Spring was a focal point for the wounded men, on both sides, during the Battle of Gettysburg (see chapter 8: First Sighting). Drinking from the spring's refreshing water was, in some cases, the last pleasurable act many of these men experienced before dying. The fierce fighting that occurred on this area of the battlefield remains vastly underestimated, but many soldiers' recollections of the combat around Spangler's Spring vividly capture its true devastation. Union Col. George Cobham of the 111th Pennsylvania Infantry described the carnage in a letter he wrote to his brother on July 4,

1863. "We have just concluded the most severe battle of the War, which has resulted in a complete victory on the Union side. The fighting has lasted two days and been desperate on both sides. All round me as I write, our men are busy burying the dead. The ground is literally covered with them and the blood is standing in pools all around me; it is a sickening sight."

Henry Hunt, Chief of Artillery in the Army of the Potomac, remembered the thick forest of hardwoods on Culp's Hill that bore the scars of the battle for many years afterward. "The scene of this conflict was covered by a forest of dead trees," he wrote in the 1880s, "leaden bullets proving as fatal to them as the soldiers whose bodies were thickly strewn beneath them."

Should you have the chance to visit, imagine what it would look like with hundreds of wounded men moaning and crying out for help. Imagine also the dead lying all around, their sightless eyes staring into the sky. If I had to choose one area on the battlefield that could provide witnesses with the best chance of experiencing a paranormal event, I would argue that Spangler's Spring is a good place to observe due to the immense suffering and bloodletting that occurred there in a relatively short period of time.

I set the camcorder on a tripod and selected a spot just in front of the spring, filming a small band of Confederate reenactors who set up a small camp behind the boulders and tree's across from Spangler's Spring and the base of Culp's Hill. My daughter Emily was with me at the time, and I filmed her hiding, jumping, and playing soldier for about three minutes. The camcorder worked great in the infrared mode at dusk. The picture possessed a slightly green tint, but otherwise the quality was excellent. Emily went over to talk with my wife Jean, who was waiting in the car, so I again focused on the reenactors. After several minutes of filming them going about their campsite routine, I moved the camera approximately ten feet to my right and began shooting the area from a different angle.

As I always do when using cameras, I noted the activity in front of the camcorder. Emily was the only person in the frame's foreground, and four or five reenactors were in the background moving around the campsite. I had a feeling that something unusual was going to happen around them. In fact, I've found that reenactors can help facilitate paranormal events, and I've used them on a number of occasions when doing experiments during investigations. When I arrived back at our hotel room, I reviewed the tape and found what I expected (and hoped) I might capture—the full apparition of a gut shot soldier!

When we replayed the footage, the form of a soldier with his back to a forked tree and his body covering the bottom front of a large boulder could be clearly defined. It remained in view for almost three minutes. It appeared as if his feet were bootless and a dark mass covered his abdomen. I intuitively believed the dark mass indicated the area of his fatal injury.

Did a ghost soldier honor me with a glimpse of how he died at Gettysburg? Did his comrades make him as comfortable as possible before heading back into the fight? The footage still has a profound impact on me. It makes me wonder what were this soldier's last thoughts. Did he think about his wife, who waited nervously for him to return home? Did his thoughts drift to his children, who had probably grown so much since he left home to fight for the cause? Or, like so many of the very young boys who died on this battlefield and never got the chance to marry and have children, perhaps he thought about his mother and the sense of comfort and safety she always provided him.

I returned the next day and took some notes at the specific location where I captured the paranormal event. I noticed in the exact spot where the apparition appeared that no dark masses were present. No large concentration of moss or leaves existed, certainly nothing the size of the dark mass in the video. And there were no logs, bushes, or tree branches in front of the boulder that could be mistaken for a person.

I knew what I captured was real and that this soldier "allowed" me to capture him on videotape, but how can I explain and make sense of it? Often on battlefields, when you visit with an open mind and heart and respect the sacrifices of the soldiers who fought there, you begin to establish a connection of sorts with the energies that remain behind. I can't describe why this happens, but I *can* say it represents the most fulfilling part of what I do. I'm capturing moments in history. I'm like a bard of old, a traveling storyteller who is privileged to have experienced special connections and who shares the stories of the fallen brave in their own words.

Chapter Eight

First Sighting

— By Jack Roth —

On May 8, 2004, I experienced what I believe to have been my first apparitional sighting as a field investigator. It occurred at a prominent location on the Gettysburg battlefield known as Spangler's Spring, where Union troops of the Twelfth Corps constructed defensive earthworks, and heavy fighting took place as both armies attempted to occupy Culp's Hill. After the war, many veterans conveyed how temporary truces were called between the sides so that men from both armies could fill their canteens with water from the spring. This particular part of the battlefield has become popular as a result of both the soldiers' anecdotes and ongoing reports of paranormal activity.

Our investigative team recorded the following testimony immediately after our strange encounter. Four individuals, including myself, who were either witness to the apparition itself or some other related phenomena share their thoughts here. Others present during the encounter are also mentioned throughout our conversation.

Many people have reported seeing both flashes and
balls of light in Spangler's Spring. Photo by Jack Roth.

"I definitely saw something moving by the tree line at the edge of the woods," I said. "It was a glowing, white object. At first, I thought it was a rock. You know how some of the rocks have a lot of white moss or bacteria covering them, so at first I thought it was a rock, but then it started moving. It was almost like it moved out from behind one of the rocks and moved back in."

"Exactly," said Sarah. "It went back in. Donna was over there and she had the same experience, and as we were all moving forward toward the object, she was moving sideways with the object. And so there was clearly, clearly something at the tree line."

"Then again it was hard because it was the gloaming time of day… dusk… and you know your eyes can play tricks on you with that type of light," I suggested. "But I really did see a glowing figure moving back and forth. And then five minutes later I saw something move again, and I went running over there because I wanted to make sure there wasn't a guy in a bright white shirt walking by or a white-tailed deer hopping along the tree line. But there was nothing like that there, so it was definitely odd."

"I was on top of the hill, and my EMF meter was going crazy," added Milo. "I was getting lots of spikes. It was funny because I thought Scott was with me. At the beginning, we were walking up the hill and I thought Scott was still next to me while we were up there. I thought he was over in the woods filming me, but I realized, 'No, there's nobody over there.' But my meter was spiking, and I felt there was somebody behind me. I got a pretty good-sized orb picture."

"The area was in between Spangler's Spring and the trail leading up to Culp's Hill, and Eric had walked that way as well," said Jon. "He said he kept feeling like there was someone behind him, and he kept looking behind his shoulder...and he kept looking like there was something up there. I felt the exact same thing. I had walked up and basically everyone else was at the bottom of the hill. I wasn't planning on going up to the top of the hill; I was planning on going about four or five turns and just standing up there because a lot of times things happen to me when there's nobody else anywhere around to verify it. So it's just my word against everyone else's. So I went up there and kept looking around. I had this feeling like I had to keep looking out, and keep on looking out because I had to make sure that you know...they weren't behind me. Eric went up just a few minutes later, and he got the same feeling."

"Right," added Milo. "I walked up the trail because Jon had just come down from there and he said that he felt like there was something up there. So I went up with my meter to see if there was something going on."

"And the interesting thing is I never told him," said Jon. "I said, 'You may want to check out further up the hill; there seems to be an electric charge or something up there.' I actually told some other people the exact same thing because I really felt like something was going to happen. I never told Milo how I felt, and then one of the first things he said when he came down was, 'I kind of feel like there's somebody back there.' It's just one of those strange things. When we first got to Gettysburg we were exhausted, but none of us had ever been here before and Jack mentioned how he felt extremely emotional for no particular reason. Melissa felt sad, and I felt like there was a drumming of energy across the entire battlefield. I've been to many active haunted houses, but this is the first time I've ever felt like an entire town and battlefield feel like one huge haunted house. It feels like there's always something going on right beneath the surface or just past the range of our senses. It's just strange … very strange to actually be walking through a large environment like that, and just not being able to feel alone at any point."

"I agree completely," I said. "This place is amazing. We may not be able to prove there was an apparition near those woods tonight, but we can certainly corroborate some pretty compelling evidence that suggests 'something' paranormal did occur. We should go back there later tonight or tomorrow morning and set up some infrared cameras."

In order to fully appreciate this account, one must first understand the spontaneous nature of apparitions. The late Andrew McKenzie, a paranormal researcher for the Society for Psychical Research (SPR), said that although members of the general public regard apparitions (or ghosts) as the spirits of the dead returning to manifest themselves to the living, it is far too simple a view of the phenomena. F. W. H. Myers, a founder of the SPR, agreed, saying that "Whatever else, indeed, a 'ghost' may be, it is probably one of the most complex phenomena in nature."

With this in mind, people must allow for the possibility that some sort of shift in consciousness occurs when experiencing a "visual" manifestation of a ghost. During most apparitional experiences, for example, the act of looking away from the apparition, even for a moment, causes the figure to disappear. McKenzie reasoned that the act of looking away might trigger a change of consciousness. In fact, most researchers generally accept that people experience apparitions in "altered states of consciousness."

Andrew Nichols, noted parapsychologist and founder of the American Institute of Parapsychology, stresses that most apparitional encounters fall into the category of "crisis apparitions," a phenomena during which people see the apparitions of friends or relatives appear before them at the very moment of the loved one's death. Such apparitions, he adds, are isolated psychic events and are usually never seen again, but if the apparition appears again and again over a long period of time, then the house (or battlefield) is considered genuinely haunted.

Regarding our experience at Spangler's Spring, we might lean toward the explanation of a genuine haunting as opposed to a crisis apparition, especially considering the location and its history. This represents a particularly compelling encounter because multiple witnesses saw the same apparition, which is very rare. Other corroborative evidence also exists, as Jon and Milo felt an electrically charged atmosphere on the path just above where and at approximately the same time the apparition was seen. Milo also recorded electromagnetic spikes on his EMF meter, which validates that some type of atmospheric anomaly was taking place.

Personally, it was a watershed moment. I never believed I would ever actually see an apparition, as years of field research had yielded many profound experiences but never an actual ghost sighting. Did we witness the genuine haunting of a restless soldier's spirit still wandering the grounds on which he experienced a violent, sudden and premature death? Or was it a replay of a battlefield moment forever etched into the environment—perhaps of a soldier cautiously emerging from the tree line in order to quench his thirst?

Either way, it seems fitting the experience occurred at Gettysburg, a place where, as Jon acutely noted, "it feels like there's always something going on right beneath the surface or just past the range of our senses."

Chapter Nine

Serenity

— By Patrick Burke —

Most paranormal experiences at Gettysburg are actually emotional in nature. Despite what many people believe, not all ghostly phenomena require audible sounds, physical manifestations, or the capture of photographic evidence in order to represent a profound or noteworthy event. In fact, simply being affected emotionally by Gettysburg's energies— whether imprinted or spirit-triggered—tends to have a more-lasting impact on people. One can only imagine the intensity and range of emotions felt by more than 150,000 soldiers and 2,400 residents both during and after the battle. As such, it isn't difficult to understand how people can be "touched" emotionally while there.

While visiting Gettysburg with my wife Jean and my oldest daughter, Emily, we took a driving tour of Culp's Hill, a fairly sizable knoll with heavily wooded slopes. Culp's Hill was occupied by Union troops for just about the entire battle despite the best efforts of the Confederates to dislodge them. This area represented the point of the famous "fishhook" in the Union line often described by historians.

Union Earthworks on Culp's Hill, where Union troops dug in against relentless Confederate attacks. Courtesy of the Library of Congress.

Jean has a degree in art history and has always been fascinated with history in general. Emily is much like her dad and finds military history to be fascinating. Jean is a sensitive, loosely defined as a person who has a high degree of proficiency in extrasensory perception or can sense or feel paranormal events beyond the range of their five human senses. Although she possesses these abilities, she doesn't actively seek to exercise them. Regardless of her wishes, sometimes the ghost soldiers just don't care. Apparently, during our visit to Culp's Hill, a young soldier wanted her to know—and feel—what happened to him, and she had no choice in the matter.

As you start up Culp's Hill, the first stone wall you come to is where the First Maryland stood its ground for the Union during a ferocious Confederate attack on the second day of fighting. Right beyond this area on

Slocum Avenue is where the first Maryland monument is located. As Maryland residents, we were very interested in checking out this site. I pulled the car over. Jean stayed in the car while Emily and I got out and approached the monument. We read each and every side of it, and I told Emily what it must have been like at this exact location on the day of the battle. We walked over to the earthworks that Union forces built to protect their strategic position on the hill.

When we got back to the car, Jean was very quiet and seemed taken aback. I asked what was wrong, and she told me the following story:

> I was just sitting here watching you and Emily walk around the monument and go over to the earthworks, and I couldn't help but think how awful it must have been. Men shooting, screaming, and dying—it was quite overwhelming. Suddenly I felt all of that chaos leave my head, and a sense of peace came over me. I looked down at the ground and saw a young soldier lying between a small rock and a tree.
>
> He was bandaged, but I knew he was dying … yet he was at peace with this fact. All of the fighting seemed to melt away from him, leaving him in this small oasis of serenity. I said a silent prayer for him and then he was gone. Then I heard you and Emily coming back to the car.

After Jean related her experience to me, I handed her my camcorder and she filmed the area in which she had the vision. There are times when a spirit wants to give you a glimpse of their life, a personal gift just for you. This was without a doubt one of those moments for Jean.

Day Two

July 2, 1863

The second day of fighting at the Battle of Gettysburg was a scorcher. The July sun beat down on the combatants and proved to be a pivotal factor in the outcome of the day's events. The actual fighting didn't start as General Lee had planned. He requested that Gen. James Longstreet and his First Corps start his attack on the Union left flank in the morning, but Longstreet decided to wait for his final brigade to arrive. Adding to the delay was the approach to his jump-off point, the point from which the attack would start. Longstreet realized halfway through the marching of his corps that the final approach would be visible to any enemy on the heights, so he turned his men around and took a different route. By the time Longstreet was in place, it was almost four p.m.

Lee intended to launch the Army of Northern Virginia in multiple attacks against the flanks of the Army of the Potomac and shear the Union defenses. Coordinated correctly, these "en echelon" attacks would force confusion in the Union lines and eventually breach it at its weakest point. Lee's plan was solid, but his lines were stretched out over a long distance, and coordinating attack would become more difficult than he anticipated. Nevertheless, the day's fighting was fierce, inflicting catastrophic casualties on both sides.

The Confederate attack started with Gen. John Bell Hood's division, and his objective was securing Little Round Top and Big Round Top—the two largest features on the battlefield. They overlooked what is now called the Valley of Death for the large number of Confederates killed crossing the valley in an attempt to drive the Union troops from the makeshift breastworks on the Round Tops. Opposite of the Round Tops was Houck's Ridge, which had the Devil's Den on its south slope, near Triangular Field.

A historical side note is needed here, as it affected the outcome of the initial action. Hood was known as a scrapper, and so were his men. He sent out some of his Texan scouts and discovered that both Round Tops were unoccupied and that the Union's entire artillery reserve was stationed behind the hills. He asked permission to change his troops position so that he could attack the rear of the Union army. Longstreet denied his request three times, stating that Lee wanted them to attack from Emmitsburg Road and that is what he intended to do. The outcome of the battle might have been different if Hood was allowed to reposition his men and attack the rear of the Union lines.

But orders were orders, and Hood started his attack, driving toward Devil's Den. As the Confederate line surged forward, they immortalized the names of the locations where the Union defenders had fought furiously to hold: the Triangular Field, Devil's Den, the Peach Orchard, the Wheatfield, the Valley of Death, Big and Little Round Top, the Codori House, Cemetery Ridge, the Bliss Farm, Cemetery Hill, and Culp's Hill.

By ten thirty p.m., the Confederate juggernaut that looked so promising during the initial attack would peter out as the men simply ran out of steam. Heat exhaustion played an important factor as the Rebel army had to do more marching and maneuvering that the Yankee defenders. The loss of life on this day was horrific. In just over five hours of fighting, a combined total of killed, wounded, and missing in action was just over 18,000 men. In other words, this means a soldier died, was wounded, or went missing in action every second!

Cemetery Ridge

ELLIOTT'S
MAP OF THE
BATTLEFIELD OF GETTYSBURG
PENNSYLVANIA

Chapter Ten

One Gallant Rush

On July 2, 1863, Confederate Gen. Robert E. Lee intended to launch the Army of Northern Virginia in multiple attacks against the flanks of the Army of the Potomac and shear the Union defenses. Coordinated correctly, these "en echelon" attacks would force confusion in the Union lines and eventually breach it. Lee's plan was solid, but his lines were stretched out over a long distance, and coordination of the attack would become more difficult than he anticipated. Nevertheless, the day's fighting was fierce, inflicting catastrophic casualties on both sides.

We decided to visit the spot where Confederate Brig. Gen. Cadmus Wilcox and his brigade of Alabamians stopped to realign before pushing to the top of Cemetery Ridge. We stood on the Confederate side of the approach to the ridge, looking at the First Minnesota Volunteer Infantry monument with its lone soldier in full stride, musket leveled. Staring at the monument, we thought what must have gone through the minds of the Confederate soldiers as they heard the Union huzza and saw the large number of Union soldiers come streaming out of the smoke toward them. And we marveled at the valor of the 262 men of the First Minnesota, a Union regiment that went into battle at the most critical time, when the Union center on this part of the field was crumbling, against a force that was six times its size.

When the smoke cleared, only 47 men from the First Minnesota returned to their original line on Cemetery Ridge.

We've been told that valor is often born of circumstance. History tells us that Union Gen. Winfield Scott Hancock saw Wilcox's brigade, unchallenged, forming near the base of a ridge with the intent of charging a gap in the Union line. Hancock knew he needed reinforcements desperately and saw the First Minnesota close at hand. He pointed to a Confederate flag over the advancing line and shouted to Col. William Colvill of the First Minnesota, "Advance, Colonel, and take those colors!"

Colvill's task was critical. If he and his men couldn't delay Wilcox's brigade from penetrating the gap before more reinforcements arrived, the Confederates would most certainly push the Union forces off their strategic position on Cemetery Ridge. If that happens, the entire Union line collapses, and the outcome of the battle is very different.

As we stood by the monument, an overwhelming sense of trepidation descended upon us. Patrick felt the words wash over him: "Dear God! Plug the gap or all is lost!" Could these have been Hancock's thoughts when he first rode up the ridge and witnessed the desperate situation unfolding before him? Did we just trigger a residual haunting? Jack must have felt something as well, as the thought still rang in our heads we paused where we stood, looking back at the monument.

The 262 men of the First Minnesota charged directly into the center of Wilcox's 1,700 Alabamians with a tremendous yell. The unit's flag fell five times and rose again each time. They momentarily stopped the Alabamians cold. Ten minutes later, the small group of surviving Minnesotans (47 men all wounded and exhausted) came streaming back as fresh Union troops came over the ridge and engaged Wilcox's brigade at the foot of the ridge. The First Minnesota's 83 percent casualty rate stands to this day as the largest loss by any surviving military unit.

General Robert E. Lee, who launched the Army of Virginia
into multiple attacks against the flanks of the Union army on
the second day of fighting. Courtesy of the Library of Congress.

Union General Winfield Scott Hancock, who ordered the
First Minnesota to stop an unchallenged Confederate assault
on Cemetery Ridge. Courtesy of the Library of Congress.

As we stood there in awe of such bravery, a woman in her forties came up beside Patrick and started talking. She noted the logo on the back of his shirt and asked if he ever investigated this battlefield. We told her about some of the evidence we captured and described some of the more personal moments we experienced on the battlefield.

She then recounted the following story to us:

I was walking in the early morning, just after sunrise, along the road just behind us. I enjoy taking brisk walks through the battlefield at that time in the morning because everything is so peaceful. As I approached the area we're standing in, I heard a great commotion. It sounded like a football game with a lot of people shouting. I couldn't see anyone around me, but it seemed to come from the area where that monument (she pointed at the First Minnesota monument) is standing. I moved closer to investigate when I heard a tremendous cheer from what seemed like hundreds of voices, and then suddenly the sounds were gone.

We asked her if she heard anything else, but she said she only remembered the shouting and especially that final cheer. It seemed so odd and out of place to her. We then described the cheer as a "hurrah" and asked her if that was close to what she heard. She believed it was.

Did she hear the cry of the First Minnesota as they charged into history? Did she hear the subsequent cheers that came from the approaching Union reinforcements who witnessed their gallant rush? Did her being in the right place at the right time allow her to experience the "living history" of an emotional event that took place on this spot over 150 years ago?

Often, the random individuals you meet while exploring Gettysburg have fascinating stories that they are more than willing to share with you. It seems they are drawn to the battlefield for one reason or another, whether they are a descendant of someone who fought in the battle or a witness to a strange paranormal event that keeps them coming back, they all have a tale to tell.

Sometimes, they represent solid eyewitnesses to paranormal phenomena, and it's important to document such stories in order to enhance the database of information that can help researchers develop patterns as to where and when certain phenomena take place.

We always return to the First Minnesota monument to see if we can witness (and capture) a part of the amazing events that took place in 1863. If nothing else, we're happy to stand and honor the men who rushed in the face of great odds and willingly sacrificed their lives for a cause in which they believed so strongly.

Chapter Eleven

A Study in Paranormal Archaeology

— By Patrick Burke —

Battlefields abound with what-ifs—those thirty-second decisions that may have changed the outcome of the battle and possibly the war. As a person who loves history, especially military history, I've always been fascinated with why the outcome of a battle happened the way it did...and at what point the tide turned? Who made the correct decision, and who was responsible for the final choice in the action?

The cool thing about being a paranormal investigator *and* a student of history is that I get to actually attempt to capture a moment in time. What were the sounds of battle, the Union huzza or the infamous rebel yell as one side or the other gains a momentary advantage, or maybe the call of the wounded pleading for help? In modern times, much of the conflict has been captured by battlefield reporters in real time. As a battlefield historian and a sensitive, I endeavor to dig down into the event on a psychic level. I can equate this with the work of archeologists as they dig through the layers of earth to discover who fought and died on the battlefield, how the fighting flowed across the land, and where the fighting was most ferocious.

Instead of digging through the soil, I dig through the historical first-hand accounts of soldiers who survived the action. In addition, I bring in people who have a psychic ability, meaning they can speak with or interact with those who have died in the action to determine if they have stayed behind or crossed over.

To do this, I bring in talented individuals whom I call investigative mediums and sensitives. Having worked in this field for years, I've developed good working relationships with a few who share my methodology and investigative approach. I always bring them in cold, and by that I mean they have no prior knowledge of the investigative site. This allows me to accurately validate the information coming in through them with the historical facts I already know. It is also helpful that, as a sensitive, I'm privy to much of the information coming to the investigative medium or sensitive.

Most paranormal investigators look at a haunting from the perspective of proving or disproving the existence or appearance of ghosts. Some research may be done on the history of the location and the people involved; it's with an eye to further the investigator's own objective. However, I believe the focus should be on validating the historical event, so I approach every investigation as a roving historical reporter. I attempt to get the spirits to interact with the investigative team and let the ghosts/spirits tell their story. When you approach an investigation from this perspective, you're actively practicing paranormal archaeology, giving yourself the ability to gather clues and information without disturbing the ground or structures around you.

Being a historian and a sensitive certainly has its advantages in the study of paranormal archaeology. As a sensitive, I ensure that I only use the information coming to me to validate the historical facts I already know. I'll let the other sensitives share what they're getting first and then add that to what I've received. Because I familiarize myself with the history of each investigative site, I can quickly ascertain if the information coming in from another sensitive or medium is correct and validate the historical event.

There's an added bonus when approaching an investigation using paranormal archaeology. Sometimes one of the team members gets a mostly unknown or hidden tidbit of information during the investigation that corroborates well-known historical facts, but it may alter our current understanding of how that particular event unfolded. You can literally rewrite the history books!

——————

My journey into paranormal archaeology began in 2004 when I was asked to come on to the *Michael Medved Show*. Yes, it was a surprise at the time, but the producer of the radio talk show said that Michael believed he had experienced a paranormal event while sleeping on Cemetery Ridge near the Copse of Trees on the Gettysburg Battlefield. In brief, Michael said that he and a friend were hitchhiking in the 1970s and got a ride to Gettysburg. It was late, so they decided to roll out their sleeping bags and sleep right on the battlefield (Back then you could get away with that!). At about two in the morning, Michael woke up, but he couldn't determine what woke him. As he sat up, he saw a glowing light around a dozen figures running on the backside of the ridge (on the south side away from the Emmitsburg Turnpike) coming toward Michael and his friend. The men were armed and he was alarmed, thinking they were in trouble. Michael realized that the figures made no sound and seemed intent on something beyond him. He shook his friend, but he was already awake and had his head in the sleeping bag. Michael watched the men coming on, realizing that the color of their uniforms were butternut and gray. He didn't share this with anyone until 2004 when the *Washington Post* did an article on my team and me. When he saw the story, he contacted me to share his personal Gettysburg paranormal event for the first time. I filed his story away, thinking it was a great experience and that I would get to share it in one of my lectures or classes.

It wasn't until 2009, when I was doing some research on known burial sites on the Gettysburg Battlefield, that I came across a piece of history not widely referenced. Made by S. G. Elliot & Company in 1864, it's called the Elliot Map. According to Elliot, the cartographer, it was an accurate survey of the battlefield grounds by transient and chain measurements. Elliott was commissioned by Congress to accurately lay out the three days' actions of the Battle of Gettysburg. He was to include the position of units before, during, and after the fight along with breastworks, lunettes, and rifle pits. He was also able to accurately place group and individual gravesites on and off the battlefield, as all of the dead were still interred in the fields. Elliot had no way of accurately measuring the number of dead in a mass grave, so he had to estimate based on interviews with townspeople who helped with the burials or the landowners where the mass gravesites were located.

It's important to understand that during the Civil War there were two ways of burying the dead. Many were buried right on the battlefield where they died in combat; these could be individual or mass graves. The soldiers who were wounded and later died in the hospitals were moved about five miles from the hospital and buried. This was done because doctors worried about disease from the dead affecting other wounded soldiers. Due to the fact that Elliot's map was created in a timely manner after the battle, and with such accuracy, he was able to precisely locate graves of soldiers and even where horses died. His map is a virtual ebb and flow of the battle.

I was looking over the map near the area called the High Watermark of the Confederacy. This is where Confederate Gen. Lewis Armistead crossed the wall near the Bloody Angle and, along with some fellow Virginians, pierced the Union line. Armistead was mortally wounded as he reached the first set of Union guns. The Elliot map showed that eighty Confederates were buried at the point where Armistead fell. This falls into line with the firsthand accounts stating that about two hundred Virginians crossed the wall with Armistead and almost half fell on the field. Elliot marked that all of the graves to the right of Taneytown Road were from hospital deaths, while those to the left of the road were buried where they fell during the battle. This was a common practice of the day.

Elliot marked thirty-six Union graves south of the Copse of Trees (COT). As I was counting the Union graves, I noticed that there were two Confederate graves just west of the COT, past the rock wall on the north slope of Cemetery Ridge. Although there are no references in any firsthand accounts, Elliot clearly indicates another six rebel graves eighty yards south of the COT, well past the Union batteries.

This caused me to sit back and think about all of the various firsthand accounts I had read about the July 2nd and 3rd day's actions around the COT. I didn't recall any account that mentioned Confederates on this part of the field, so I looked through my notes from my many visits to that part of the battlefield. Although I felt the presence of Confederates around various spots near the COT, I assumed they were just residual energies from the third day's action or what I call "walk-through" ghosts (meaning spirits that are just passing through).

Looking at the map again, I noticed that there were thirty-three individual Confederate graves about 200 yards south of the COT and approximately 250 yards west of Meade's headquarters. The Elliot Map shows two structures at this location, and they're still there today. Whoa! I thought, *What the hell is this?!* Like so many of the soldiers who died on this battlefield, these Confederates would have been buried where they fell during combat, and this spot was well behind the Union defensive lines.

Continuing to reference the Elliot Map, I counted sixty-nine Union graves between the six Confederate graves south of the COT and the thirty-three additional Confederate graves in the field at the Leister House. There are also another ten Union soldiers buried on the north side of Taneytown Road, just beyond the two structures west of Meade's headquarters.

Accepted historical accounts tell us the High Watermark of the Confederacy is just east of the COT, where General Armistead was mortally wounded on the third day of the battle. However, the Elliot Map clearly indicates the presence of Confederate soldiers where history tells us they shouldn't have been. This map is worthy of serious consideration because it was commissioned by the U. S. Congress and completed within a year after the battle. At that time, eyewitnesses were still alive, the scars on the landscape were still evident, and the graves were still clearly visible. This area between the crest of Cemetery Ridge and the almost 200 yards to Taneytown Road obviously saw some serious action. This is a location where common history tells us no fighting took place!

Then I recalled my interview with Michael Medved, his story, and his location on the battlefield. Combining his story with the information on the map, I felt strongly that it was time to investigate his haunting experience and how it might be tied to the battlefield graves on the Elliot Map. So many questions popped into my head. Why would there be a residual haunting of Confederate soldiers where, by all historical accounts, they never were? Why, when soldiers were buried where they fell, are there Confederate graves beyond what current historical accounts call the High Watermark of the Confederacy? These were the nagging questions that led me to begin my journey into paranormal archaeology.

From my research pertaining to the third day of the battle, I knew that no large force of Confederates had been in the area where Michael saw the ghost soldiers. I started reading through the Official Report of the second day's action. Among these, I came across Brig. Gen. Ambrose Wright's (CSA) Official Report in which he stated, as a matter of fact, that his brigade not only took the Union position where more than sixteen cannons had blasted away at the Confederate advance on Cemetery Ridge, but they had also split the Federal defensive line.

What an eye-opener! If this actually happened, why didn't the Confederates seize the foothold gained and expand upon it? Assuming that Wright did in fact accomplish what he claimed, I wanted to know what caused the failure of the breach? History tells us that the Union defenders fought off the bold Confederate advance, which led to Trimble and Pickett's charges on the third day.

I diligently began my walk into paranormal archaeology. I began combing through as many firsthand accounts of this particular action as I could find and the various regimental histories and letters of recollections. I visited the National Archives to look over maps and period photos, reading all of the field reports and official reports of the engagement that were available.

Jack and I incorporate psi talent to help define the gaps in history, or the deliberate omission of historical facts. My objective was to, once and for all, establish the validity of Wright's claim that "We were masters of the field." Wright's Official Report is a subject that is controversial with historians, armchair generals, and military enthusiasts alike. The question is whether or not General Wright and his men actually penetrated the Union line of defense on Cemetery Ridge during the second day of the Battle of Gettysburg, as he states in his Official Report after the battle.

Here is a brief description of what took place:

General Wright was to launch his attack on the center of the Union line dug in on Cemetery Ridge when Gen. Edward Perry's Brigade of Floridians started off on his right flank. On cue, Wright moved his line forward. The Confederates stepped off smartly, as if on parade, moved past the Bliss Farm on its far left, crossing over the Emmitsburg Turnpike. They drove the Eighty-Second New York and then the Fifteenth Massachusetts from their positions around the Codori House. Lt. Fred Brown's Battery B from Rhode Island continued firing (even wounding and killing some of the Union infantry by accident) until the last minute.

As the Federal troops and Brown's Battery retreated to the stone wall at the base of Cemetery Ridge, Wright's brigade followed hot on their heels. The fight at the stone wall was fierce. Brown was able to get four (according to Sgt. John Rhodes of Battery B only three) of his six guns behind the waiting infantry, and the other two pieces now belonged to Wright. Lt. Alonzo Cushing's Battery A, Fourth US Light Artillery turned their guns on the two pieces to keep the Confederates off of them. As the Eighty-Second New York and the Fifteenth Massachusetts streamed through the gap in the stone wall, they re-formed behind the batteries on Cemetery Ridge, which were supported by the Sixty-Ninth and 106th Pennsylvania troops behind the stone wall.

Here, General Wright, under heavy cannon and musket fire, re-formed his lines and charged into the teeth of the dragon. He captured several batteries during the charge and drove off the Union infantry defending the ridge. He was master of the field, but for only a brief time as Union reinforcements arrived on his flanks and in front of him. With no support in sight, he withdrew to a small swale several hundred yards away.

The controversy is centered on whether General Wright's brigade actually crested the ridge. All of the Union accounts I've read so far indicate that the Confederates never gained the heights, but rather that they penetrated the first line of defense on the west side of the ridge and were stopped just before approaching the top. All of the Southern accounts claim that he did gain the heights and by so doing split the Federal defenses in half.

So how can we use the method of paranormal archaeology to solve this dispute? It should be noted that, in the majority of cases, the Confederate officers tended to give a more accurate description when writing their reports than their Union counterparts. For instance, when the Confederate troops were routed, the Offical Report says they were routed. The Union reports of a rout usually have the following words: fell back in good order or maintained cohesion as they retreated to a second line of defense. In all honesty, no one, Rebel or Yankee, wanted to admit that his troops fell back in disarray.

So, here are the facts as we know them: General Wright's brigade did indeed drive back the Union defenses around the Codori House, seizing one gun there, regrouping in front of the stone wall, and taking two of Brown's guns that had been left behind at the wall.

This is supported by a number of accounts: Wright's Official Report, Brown's Official Report, and Charles H. Andrews's History of the Third Georgia (he was the Company Regimental Historian). His is the most detailed when it comes to the actual action that took place at company levels, and I generally consider it closer to the truth than any other report. The following is an excerpt from his accounts:

"The Third Georgia moved forward and was met at the edge of the field in front with a storm of shot and shell. At a double quick step, the Regiment charged upon the enemy in the turnpike, followed at their heels across the little meadow beyond, passed a large brick house…"

General Wright gives a similar account of what happened at the Codori farmhouse and Lt. Col. George Joslin (US) of the Fifteenth Massachusetts also verifies this account. Although Joslin does give a unique point of view, he states that the Fifteenth Massachusetts was positioned to the left of the Eighty-Second New York and that the Fifteenth built a small breastwork when the pressure was such that the men broke and ran for the stone wall where the Sixty-Ninth and 106th Pennsylvania infantry were hunkered down. Note how he describes the retreating Fifteenth Massachusetts, which was in all actuality, a rout. It should be noted that the Eighty-Second New York was routed as well.

Joslin writes, "At this time the Eighty-Second New York fell back, exposing our left and rear to a deadly fire from the rebel infantry. Here Colonel Ward received wounds from which he has since died. We now opened a rapid fire, but being left alone could hold the position but a short time, when we retired in some disorder, being pressed so closely that we lost quite a number of prisoners, captured by the enemy. We reformed our line in rear of the batteries, and rejoined the brigade, which was moved after dark to the front line…"

The most telling factor is that Joslin doesn't even reference the fighting at the stone wall. If the Fifteenth Massachusetts had regrouped just behind the batteries on top of Cemetery Ridge, he would have been in a position to witness this engagement. I made a note to enquire of any ghost soldiers of the Fifteenth Massachusetts whose energies still reside on the battlefield to tell me where they reformed.

Most interesting about this is the lack of information from the Union officers pertaining to the details of the action at the stone wall and the guns on the ridge. For instance, Union Gen. Alexander Webb states that the Confederates made it past one of Brown's guns and then were driven back as the Seventy-First and Seventy-Second Pennsylvania advanced to the support of the Sixty-Ninth and 106th Pennsylvania. According to General Webb, Wright's brigade only advanced to one of Brown's guns. Which gun was it? According to Sergeant Rhodes of Brown's Battery B, Brown left one gun at the Codori House and had two more stuck at the stone wall. The remainder of Brown's Battery joined Battery A on the ridge and opened fire at the approaching Confederates.

We know from previous reports that Wright's brigade took the Codori House and made it to the stone wall. In Wright's Official Report he states:

"I immediately charged upon the enemy's line, and drove him in great confusion upon his second line, which was formed behind a stone fence, some one hundred or more yards in rear of the Emmitsburg Turnpike. At this point we captured several pieces of artillery, which the enemy in his haste and confusion was unable to take off the field."

From this description, we know that Joslin's account is fairly accurate in that both Wright and Joslin reported the capturing of field pieces. Although Wright indicates that several were captured, we will go with the conservative number of one gun captured.

That Wright broke the Union line at the wall there is no doubt, as all accounts claim this. The issue is whether Wright took the crest of Cemetery Ridge and, in doing so, seized the guns on the heights and split the Union defense in two. As I continued to research, I came across a reference to the second day of the battle written by Gen. Henry J. Hunt, Chief of Artillery of the Army of the Potomac during the battle, for *The Century* magazine. He wrote three articles dated November 1886, December 1886, and January 1887, respectively. Read, in his own words, what Hunt had to say about the conflict at Cemetery Ridge, and pay close attention to the final sentence:

> The first assaults were repulsed, but, after hard fighting, McLaws' division being also advanced, the angle was, toward six o'clock, broken in, after a resolute defense and with great loss on both sides. In the mean time three of Anderson's brigades were advancing on Humphreys, and the latter received orders from Birney, now in command of the corps, Sickles being severely wounded soon after six o'clock near the Trostle house, to throw back his left, form an oblique line in his rear, and connect with the right of Birney's division, then retiring. The junction was not effected, and Humphreys, greatly outnumbered, slowly and skillfully fell back to Cemetery Ridge, Gibbon sending two regiments and Brown's Rhode Island battery to his support. But the enemy was strong and covered the whole Second Corps front, now greatly weakened by detachments. Wilcox's, Perry's, and Wright's brigades pressed up to the ridge, outflanking Humphreys's right and left, and Wright broke through our line and seized the guns in his front, but was soon driven out, and not being supported all fell back, about dusk, under a heavy artillery fire.

Hunt is describing Wright's breakthrough at the ridge, and his reference to the seizing of the guns is very clear. If Wright had captured one or two guns, Hunt would have given us that exact number or would have used the common reference of several guns or pieces of artillery. The only guns in Wright's front, at this stage of the fighting, were the ones on Cemetery Ridge. This is corroboration supporting the first claim of Wright's Official Report that he took the guns on the ridge. But, how do we prove the second part of Wright's claim that his brigade "was a now complete master of the field"?

In June 2012, Jack and I decided to do an investigation of the various points of engagement of Wright's brigade on Day Two. I brought both of my daughters, Emily and Shannon, who are both talented sensitives and have only a cursory knowledge of the battle. The goal was to use our combined psi talent to communicate with the ghost soldiers and get to the heart of the issue.

Jack and I parked just south of Meade's Headquarters in a field lot on Taneytown Road. I wanted to see if we could find the remains of the ravine just south of Meade's HQ. Wright mentions a ravine to the east of his position on Cemetery Ridge. Jack and I started to walk down Taneytown Road with the map and came to a creek bed on the left side of the road. Looking at the map, I heard a voice say, "Over here!" I turned and saw a cannon standing upright with the muzzle buried in the ground. As Jack studied the map, I crossed the street to look at the plate on the cannon and caught my breath … the marker indicated that the location of Hunt's HQ was before me, just south of Meade's HQ. I stepped up beside the monument and turned to look at the backside of Cemetery Ridge, realizing that Hunt would have had a perfect view of Wright's troops as they crested the ridge, waving their battle flags in assumed victory. I called Jack and said "I found Hunt's HQ! He had a firsthand view of the final actions of Wright's brigade."

We walked back to the car and opened the Elliot Map. Our next objective was to locate the two structures just south of Meade's HQ and conduct our investigation of the field at the base of Cemetery Ridge. Elliot indicated that there were thirty-three Confederate soldiers buried in this field as well as ten Union graves. This is the area where we would be able to prove or disprove Wright's claims, as this would be the furthest the Confederates would have gone before being turned back.

We pulled into a parking area by the structures. A park ranger happened to be there, and I asked him for permission to walk out on the field as I was curious about the accuracy of the Elliot Map. He replied that he knew of the map and that it was accurate; there had been multiple graves in that field. I thanked him and felt a surge of excitement as I walked over to the team. "This is the spot!"

I instructed Emily and Shannon to go through the training I had taught them, basically putting up psi shields against negative energies and opening up their psi abilities to the zero-point field (ZPF). It's important to note that Jack is critical of using the information provided only by sensitives to assess what may have occurred at a particular location. In this case, he was excited because we had the map and we had multiple battle reports that we could use to verify whatever the girls came up with from a psi standpoint. He also trusts my methods and knows from experience that I have a sincere connection to ghost soldiers. Ironically, Jack has unwillingly developed his own psi abilities simply by being around paranormal energies over the years, and his paranormal intuition has been extremely helpful in assessing particular situations at haunted locations.

I lead the team toward the break in the fence and the uncut field beyond. I stopped at the opening in the fence and was hit with the unmistakable feeling of many eyes watching us. "Boys," I said quietly, "My name is Patrick and I have with me Jack, Emily, and Shannon. We are here to ask you about what happened here on July 2, 1863. We are hopeful that you will share with us a bit of your story... your name, rank, or regiment and company you were with during the fighting that happened here on July 2nd."

A brief image flashed in my head. Soldiers in butternut and gray forming a quick line and firing at a thin line of Union soldiers with the haze of battle thick on the field, and then a rolling crash of musketry off to the left of the Confederates and then... the clear blue skies of the present.

Jack stepped past us, and Emily said, "They're still out there," and pointed toward the field before us.

I looked at her, already knowing the answer but asking it anyway, "Who?"

Shannon said, "The soldiers." I looked at her as Emily said, "There are bodies still out there." I felt a shiver run through my spine. The girls were already getting a stream of information, and they were completely unaware of the events that unfolded in this area. Jack and I told and showed them nothing before starting the investigation. Plus, this was information I was also receiving but hadn't shared with them yet.

As we worked our way into the field, I let Emily and Shannon guide us to the location where the ghost soldiers had indicated their bodies were. As they were walking, Shannon suddenly stopped and said, "Here!" This precise area was the area where Elliott indicated Confederate and Union soldiers had fallen in battle and been buried. Emily mentioned that a Union soldier was approaching her. She believed his name was Daniels, and I asked her to inquire about his rank. She said he had stripes. She wasn't sure but thought he was a sergeant. He indicated to her that he was with a Massachusetts regiment and that he came from the north (from their position at the Codori House). Shannon said, "From that direction," (she was pointing north toward Cemetery Ridge), and "had fallen back to this spot." I was confident this was a live interaction with the spirit of Daniels.

I was excited to garner this information because Daniels corroborated that a Massachusetts unit had fallen back to the base of Cemetery Ridge. But was it the Fifteenth? If we could determine that information, maybe it would explain why Joslin's report lacked the details regarding this action. He would have been busy rallying his remaining men in the field near the Leister House.

"Are you Confederates?" Emily asked, already knowing the answer, but wanting to validate it for us to hear. "No." "Did you retreat to this spot?" "Yes." Then Emily said an "aide" was with them from General "H," but she couldn't make out the name. I asked Shannon if she could make out the name and she thought it sounded like "Han." I then asked if the name was Hancock, and the girls and Jack said "Yes!" "I went with the first thing that came into my head, and that was Hancock," Jack said. "I'm just flowing with this." I laughed. I knew from past investigations that Jack was quite good at this. He just didn't fully trust that he could actually do it.

Emily said a Confederate soldier named George was standing near me. I asked him who his commanding general was. "Anderson," Emily said. R. H. Anderson was the commanding general for that division. When asked what rank he was, Emily replied, "Captain." When I prompted Emily to request what regiment he was with she held up two fingers. Research confirms that Capt. George Salley Jones of the Second Georgia Battalion was wounded on Cemetery Ridge.

Again, we had most likely just validated that elements of Wright's brigade not only seized the cannons on the ridge but also had gone more than 200 yards past the ridge line, almost reaching Taneytown Road.

As is sometimes the situation, when the ghost soldiers realize that there is someone on hand that they can communicate with them the conversation can turn into a chorus of voices saying various things. This is what happened when I said that many Union accounts state the boys from Wright's brigade never took the guns on the heights. Shannon laughed and shook her head as Emily cried out, "No, no, no! Third Georgia, we took them. Took two, left two!" Emily said there were a lot of men, even men in blue, that said they took the guns, but the Union soldiers were quick to point out they got them back.

I then asked how they stopped the Confederates and Emily drew a line in front of her. "The Fifteenth Massachusetts re-formed here, and as they engaged the Confederates, another company of Union soldiers came around from that direction," and she pointed toward Meade's headquarters. This information coincided with the image I had received at the fence line before entering the field and with Wright's own report.

Shannon asked if we could cross over the soldiers that wanted to move on. I felt that we had successfully gathered credible evidence, both historical and paranormal, that allowed us to verify and validate that Wright's brigade did, in fact, do what he claimed and seize the guns on Cemetery Ridge, causing the Union defenses to split. I told her it was now time for us to assist the soldiers to their final rest.

When doing a crossover of a spirit, it is important to understand that in many cases it is easier to assist the spirit by communicating in the terms that they understood when they were alive and use whatever terms for whatever higher being they believe in. This sometimes makes individuals uncomfortable, I understand that. What those individuals also need to understand, whether they believe in the psychic abilities of others or that spirits can be crossed over, is that as a sensitive we do feel the need of the soul to be at peace and in all cases in which the spirit is asking for aid it is imperative that we assist when we can.

I briefly walked Emily and Shannon through the process as I normally do and asked the spirits if they were ready to go. I heard the Union and Confederate soldiers say, "Not together." Emily said, "Daniels says let the Confederates go first; they don't want to go together." I said it wasn't a problem and set to work.

I connected my energy field to Emily and Shannon's and then opened the portal through the zero-point field. The stream of energy was intense. As the Confederate soldiers approached, Emily asked them to give us a rebel yell as they crossed over. Twenty-six soldiers crossed over and I couldn't believe the intensity of the rebel yell that washed over us. I had heard the rebel yell before, but not like this. The hair on my arms was standing straight up!

The Union boys stepped up after the Confederates had passed over. Daniels and his Union comrades wanted to make sure their story would be told and people would know what happened. I assured them that we would share their story and do what we could to locate the graves and have the dead honored. Twelve Union soldiers crossed over with a huzzah washing over us.

As we left the field, Jack said he felt a quietness that was not there before. We stood near the house on Taneytown Road and looking back into the field we talked about the information that we just gathered in the investigation. I felt that we had successfully gathered credible evidence, both historical and paranormal. This allowed us to verify and validate that Wright's brigade did, in fact, do what Wright claimed and seize the guns on Cemetery Ridge, causing the Union defenses to split.

As the information came in, the picture became clearer. The advancement of Wright's brigade on the second day of the battle went much farther than even I had imagined, almost 200 to 300 yards beyond the crest of Cemetery Ridge. With the aid of the girl's psi abilities, Jack and I were able to validate the documented historical information and paint a complete picture of the last moments of the Confederacy's farthest advance. As we looked at each other, we realized we were standing on what was the true High Water Mark of the Confederacy.

———

After reviewing the evidence, I told Jack I was going to call my good friends Shawn Taylor and Dan Morgan. They have been leading the way in developing a system for live communication with those who have passed on that they call "The Double-Blind Ghost Box" (*The Double-Blind Ghost Box*, Shawn Taylor and Dan Morgan, iUniverse, Inc. 2013).

I had worked with Shawn and Dan on an investigation of the Otto Farm, part of the battle of Sharpsburg/Antietam, and was impressed with their professionalism and attention to detail. The basic concept of a ghost box is to use a random AM radio frequency to enable the ghosts to communicate with you more easily. You ask a question and then listen for an answer. The problem with this method is that everyone present hears the questions, allowing for people perceiving tainted answers based on what they know the question is.

What Shawn and Dan did was take this process to the next level. They created a system in which there is a Questioner and a Listener. The Listener is connected to the ghost box via high-quality, noise-reduction headphones with the volume on high, making them unable to hear anything except the sounds coming through the ghost box. Additionally, the Listener is turned away to look at the ground or a wall, never looking at the Questioner and avoiding any possibility of reading lips. The Questioner also stands about twenty-five feet away from the Listener to further ensure no words are overheard.

The experiment begins when the Questioner asks a question out loud. If there is a medium in the room, he or she should be out of the Listener's sight and give their answer before the Listener does. Next, the Listener gives an answer. If the Listener, alone, gets the correct response, you have accomplished the highly improbable. If the medium has given the same answer first, you may have achieved the statistically impossible. This systematic, organized approach minimizes the uncontrolled variables.

Jack and I totally agree that this technique and methodology are as valid as can be when dealing with psi experiments. To further support the investigative findings, the Listener has a digital recorder plugged into the ghost box along with the headphones. This allows the sounds form the ghost box to be reviewed and validated by the investigators. The Questioner holds a camcorder and a digital recorder, as well. The entire session is captured by multiple media sources and from multiple perspectives. The investigators mark the recordings and video so they can sync audio and video together after the investigation.

To experiment with this, I arranged to meet the guys and their team at Gettysburg for three days. They brought three teams: Team 1—Shawn and Dan; Team 2—Amy Buchanan and Shelley Smith; Team 3—David Hendricks and Jim Johnson. I brought my sister, Mary Russell, a talented medium in her own right who has worked with Jack and me on several other investigations. Kenny Coombs acted as team photographer. My goal was to control the information coming through to each group and Mary. I gave them the name of the hotel and told them that everyone would be briefed at the same time. No specific information about the battle was provided.

I had Chris Carouthers and Karen Mitchell-Carouthers scheduled to meet me at the knoll between the Codori House and the stone wall where the Eighty-Second New York and Fifteenth Massachusetts Infantry had been posted. This slight rise is where Brown's Battery B Rhode Island Light Artillery was located with six Napoleon guns in support of the Eighty-Second New York and the Fifteenth Massachusetts. These two regiments were ordered to move forward and occupy the ground at the Codori House.

I decided to focus on Wright's approach from the point where he claimed to capture several pieces of Brown's battery at the knoll and then as he re-formed to charge the wall at the base of Cemetery Ridge. From this point, I needed to know what path Wright's brigade took, so I had Dave and Jim work the area from the wall between the Fifteenth Massachusetts and Eighty-Second New York monuments and up the crest of the ridge to the right of the Copse of Trees (west). To validate the information gathered earlier during the investigation Emily, Shannon, Jack, and I conducted in the open field by the two structures just south of Meade's and Hunt's HQ near Taneytown Road, I had Amy and Shelley dress in period dresses. They walked the boulder-strewn field on the backside of Cemetery Ridge and worked their way down toward the area where the thirty-three Confederates were buried. At the knoll, Shawn and Mary were the Listeners, Dan and I were the Questioners and Mary did an area read. I asked Shawn if we could hook up two Listeners to see what would happen if a medium was also attached to the ghost box system. He rigged up another set of headphones and we were ready to go.

We began the investigation at the Knoll. I started off by asking the ghost soldiers to interact with us. "Hey boys, I'm here with my good friends to try and accurately recount the fighting that took place here on July 2, 1863. You can communicate directly with Mary, me, or Shawn. We just want to capture a bit of your story to make sure that history has been told correctly. If it hasn't, we will correct it."

I felt a heaviness in the area, as if an unseen hand was pressing on the back of my head, a sure sign that a lot of energy was present. As Mary crossed over the stone wall between the Fifteenth Massachusetts and the Eighty-Second New York monuments, I asked where Brown's guns got stuck. Dan, Shawn, and Mary were walking several yards in front of me, just clearing the wall when Mary pointed to her left and said, "To my left." She pointed toward the Fifty-Ninth New York monument where historical records indicate that two of Brown's guns had been stuck while trying to clear the gap in the wall at the same time. This started a string of contact with Dan asking questions and Mary and Shawn calling out what they heard. As I reached the position of the battery, I started to feel anxious. Urgency seemed to be all around me, as if something was terribly wrong. About fifteen feet away from me, Shawn said, "What's wrong. Help!" Dan asked the ghost soldier what his name was and Mary replied, "Richard."

I had the feeling that there was an issue with Brown's cannons. Suddenly, I heard very clearly, "Wrong direction!" And then I heard Mary say something about "The right direction." Could Brown have positioned his Battery in the wrong direction? What effect would that have had when he fired as Wright's brigade approached? After the investigation, I did further research on Brown's battery and came across a video series by licensed Battlefield Guide George Newton. Newton stated that when Brown set up his battery of six Napoleon guns, he positioned them in what is called a right oblige, meaning he had his cannons facing to the northwest. This means Brown's battery was facing away from the approach of Wright's brigade, who was approaching from the Codori House to the west. Wright advanced so fast that Brown could only get several cannons turned in time to have any effect on the approaching Confederates.

Imagine you were one of the gunners in Brown's unit, or even Brown himself. What a shock it must have been to suddenly realize that all of your cannons were facing in the wrong direction! The pandemonium that ensued must have been something to observe. For any of Brown's guns to get off any rounds is a testament to those brave soldiers' ability to do their job under extreme circumstances. At this knoll, Brown would lose two of his guns, have three men killed, seventeen men wounded and one man captured. Brown himself was struck in the neck by a bullet.

I proceeded to ask a series of questions about the location of certain regiments on Wright's brigade during the fighting. "Where is the Second Georgia Battalion?" Mary said "left" and pointed to the area where the Second Georgia secured the right flank of Wright's brigade. Chris then came over and asked if there was a James or a colonel whose first name started with a J. I asked him to give me a last name and he said "Wasden." He felt as if he couldn't breathe and then pointed to the Codori House in the distance saying, "He died there, right?" Col. Joseph Wasden, commander of the Twenty-Second Georgia, was killed and buried on the grounds of the Codori House as shown on the Elliott Map.

Chris then began to feel extreme anxiety and worry because there was no support for the Confederates advancing. I heard Mary say "Richard" again and Chris say, "He sent a message to Anderson." Richard H. Anderson was the divisional commander and Wright, in his report, states that he sent three messages to him asking for his support.

The level of validation of the historical facts was outstanding. Using the double-blind ghost box method ensured that those answering the questions were doing so with no knowledge of the questions being asked, and the answers they gave were spot-on.

I moved the team about 100 feet before the location of Brown's battery because I wanted to see if I could locate the Third Georgia's approach. I got on the ghost box with Shawn and, immediately, we both said "three" and then I said "third." I then asked, "When they reached this spot did they think they had held the day?" Shawn replied, "Stacked." Could that have been a reference to the Twenty-Second Georgia crowding the Third Georgia because the Second Georgia became mixed into the Twenty-Second Georgia's lines? At this point, I slipped in a trick question to see what would happen. "Did the Fourteenth Mississippi go forward with you?" If the answer was yes, then I knew the information might be tainted because the Forty-Eighth Mississippi is the only regiment from Posey's brigade that went forward with Wright's men. Shawn quickly said, "Not the right question, Burke!" Obviously the ghost soldier knew that I had asked a misleading question and also knew my name. This systematic, organized approach minimizes the uncontrolled variables. Very cool indeed.

I moved up to the wall where the Union soldiers of the Eighty-Second New York and the Fifteenth Massachusetts retreated. At that spot, Dave Hendricks was the Listener and Jim Johnson was asking questions. They had been working this area with the intent to gather validation of action that took place here and to see if they could pinpoint Wright's breakthrough at the wall. They started at the Knoll with Jim asking where Wright's brigade took the guns. Dave called out, "Hold, brother!" Jim was standing near Brown's Battery marker. They moved to the wall and, while crossing over near the Fifteenth Massachusetts monument, Dave said he was getting a cramp in his abdomen as if he had been shot. The ghost box recorded the following, "He's hurt … He died."

When asked if the Eighty-Second New York could point out where the Fifteenth Massachusetts was, the response was a surprising, "They left!" According to Joslin's report of the Fifteenth Massachusetts, the Eighty-Second New York broke first, which caused the Fifteenth to fall back. Then Dave called out, "Fall back!" Jim asked if any shots were fired, to which the reply was, "Yes, sir!" Jim, who wasn't on the ghost box, heard some reenactors fire their muskets in the distance and asked if they sounded like that, and a ghost soldier said, "We looked better." Jim called roll call for the Fifteenth Massachusetts. Jack and I regularly do this on a battlefield as a way to prompt any ghost soldiers who are present to respond. We usually select names of soldiers who died at the location or were wounded, throwing in a name or two of soldiers we know weren't there to see what happens. "Roll call!" said Jim. Dave suddenly called out, "We're listening"—"1st Sergeant Henry C. Ball"—"Brother." Could this be a reference to a brother in arms? 1st Sgt. Henry C. Ball died during the second day's action. At this point, Dave was standing about halfway up Cemetery Ridge with the Copse of Trees off to his right. He said, "I need to know where Wright's brigade broke the line." "Back!" came through. Dave started walking back toward the wall as Jim asked where Wright's brigade broke through. Dave was walking about halfway between the New York and Massachusetts monuments when he stopped and called out the answer to their query, "Was here!"

Jim asked about the fighting: Any shots or wounded? How bad was the fighting? Any New York regiments? Dave then called out a string of replies: "Wounded"—"Rescued . . . Bad!"—"Here!'—"Battle." This session with the ghost soldiers from the Eighty-Second New York and the Fifteenth Massachusetts reinforced the historical information we already know. Did they fall back from the Codori House to the position at the wall, make a brief stand, and then retire behind the guns on the ridge? Dave and Jim were able to verify that Wright's men had broken the Union defenses at the wall, and now all I had to do was confirm, through the words of the ghost soldiers themselves, if Wright had seized the guns on the top of Cemetery Ridge.

I asked Amy Buchanan and Shelley Smith to wear period dresses since they both are active reenactors. I wanted to see how the ghost soldiers would react to women, not only on the battlefield, but also in period dress. Jack and I have made it a common practice to incorporate, when possible, reenactors in period dress and uniform. Our observations suggest that the amount of activity around the reenactors tends to be more. Using the ghost box, Amy was the Questioner and Shelley the Listener. They started just inside the field, which is near the top of the ridge on the south slope of Cemetery Ridge. From this location, you can see the Leister house and the big red barn on the property, in addition to the field where we had done an earlier investigation.

Amy asked, "General Wright, are you here?" The answer was immediate: "I was…time to go!" Amy and Shelley appeared to have brought out the ghost soldiers rather quickly. Amy asked, "How many men are here?" and the reply was "Sixteen—Now—We're here!" They were able to get a name when Amy asked for one. Shelley said, "Colt." Amy then asked if that was his last name and the reply was, "Yes."

Upon further review of the recording, it was determined that the name given was either Cole or Clarke.

I later researched the list of dead to see if a Colt or Cole had been present with any of Wright's brigade on July 2, 1863. I came across a Private J. M. Cole of Company C of the Twenty-Second Georgia. I then went back to Charles H. Andrews' account of the second day's action, and Cole was present at the fighting on Cemetery Ridge where Wright claimed to seize the guns and split the Union line. As I stated earlier in this chapter, Andrews described how the fighting developed around the Codori Farm. His account further stated that the Third Georgia stormed the wall and took command of the thirteen cannons on the ridge. He said that during the fighting, he was standing next to a man named Clarke from Company D "who was killed while sitting astride a cannon loading and shooting." Research shows that Private Rueben W. L. Clarke of Company D was killed on the second day of the battle. Then, surprisingly, we heard, "Touch Amy?" This indicates that this ghost soldier was aware of his surroundings and the people in the area, meaning a direct interaction was taking place. Could this be Private Cole?

Shelley said she heard cannon fire and called out a string of EVP: "They come quick!—Yes they do!" Amy asked if they could stop the cannon firing and the response Shelley received was, "There is someone behind you!— Sitting in front." When asked what was in front of them, the reply was "Humphreys."

Historical records indicate that elements of the First Brigade commanded by Brig. Gen. Joseph B. Carr of Humphrey's Division would have been within sight and may have been in front of some of the men of Wright's brigade's right flank as the Second Georgia Battalion and the Twenty-Second Georgia advanced up the slope. Amy called out roll call: "Pvt. J. M. Baker, are you here?" Listening on the ghost box, Shelley answered "*Yeah.*" "Pvt. J. W. Gorvie, are you here?" "That's me—Hi!" "Robert W. Rutherford are you here?" "Died." "Col. E. J. Walker (commander of the Third Georgia), are you here?" "No!" was the surprising answer. Amy followed up with, "Where is he—If not here where is he?" "He's happy." Amy then asked, "Why?" Shelley looked really surprised and said she was hearing many voices singing, as if a choir of angels was performing.

I joined Amy and Shelley as they were coming back up through the field toward the top of Cemetery Ridge. I stood off to the side and observed their interaction with the ghost soldiers through the double-blind ghost box method. Amy got Shelley's attention and pointed out that a group of Union reenactors was marching with the flags. These men, who carried the flags and the guards with them, are referred to as the Color Guard. Amy spotted them on the road at the top of Cemetery Ridge. The Color Guard was just even with the Copse of Trees heading toward the large Pennsylvania monument. Amy recognized that they would be moving directly through the area that Wright's brigade had occupied and she suggested that we can use that to our advantage. I nodded my head in agreement, wondering how the Georgia boys would react to the Union reenactors marching their colors through this area.

As Amy finished talking and moved toward the reenactors, the ghost box came alive. I felt a surge of energy in the area, as if a large group of men were hurrying to stop a flood. Shelley started to call out what she heard. "Bring it!" one soldier cried out. As they moved closer to the Color Guard, a number of voices called out, "Run them off!—Burn 'em up!" Shelley had no idea what questions Amy was asking as she called out a string of answers. Amy asked: "Do you want to run the North off? Get the Yankees?" "Kill 'em!"—"Go after these Yankees?"—"Shoot, damn it! Take a shot!" As the reenactors passed the Copse of Trees, Amy asked, "What are the orders…orders?" "Hurry!"—"The Yankees are coming!"—"Shoot 'em!…Move!…Go!"—"Do you see the Yankees?"—"Yeah." Upon review of the ghost box audio, you can hear men fighting in the background when these answers were given. After this exchange, there was a pause and Shelley called out the words from a ghost soldier, "They're hunting." Hunting is a term used when the enemy's line has been broken, they are in retreat and now the soldiers are looking to pick off any stragglers or anyone wounded that might still be a threat.

As I was listening to Shelley calling out what she heard from the ghost box, I thought, "Is this the point where Confederate Brig. Gen. Ambrose Wright had to make his fateful decision…to hold and possibly lose his command while waiting for support he knew in his heart wasn't coming, or to give the order to retreat and save what was left of his command? With her intuition in full swing, Amy asked the final question.

"General Wright will you give the order?" Suddenly a man's agonized reply, "No!" I asked Amy what she was thinking when she asked that final question and she told me she wanted to know if he would give the order to charge the oncoming Yankees.

As I stood there, an image of heavy, thick smoke rolling over the area with men seemed to move in slow motion surround me. Then it exploded into fast motion. The butternut and gray holding the ridge and the field beyond, the Rebels streaming back as the Union countercharged and began to envelop the Rebel flanks. Just as suddenly, it was gone, but it had taken my breath away. I knew without a doubt that Wright's brigade had accomplished what Wright had claimed, "We were now complete masters of the field …"

After reviewing the historical evidence, the Official Reports, firsthand accounts, letters of recollection, and then tying in the paranormal evidence from the various investigations, a clear picture has developed:

On July 2, 1863, just around six p.m., the brigade of Gen. Ambrose Wright of R. H. Anderson's Division stepped off from their assigned position toward the Codori House. At the Codori House, the Fifteenth Massachusetts and the Eighty-Second New York gave brief resistance and then retired from the field, streaming past Brown's Battery on the slight rise in front of the stone wall at the north base of Cemetery Ridge. Wright pushed his men forward, hot on the heels of the retreating Union soldiers. Lieutenant Brown waited until the last minute to fire his guns and pull them back. During this action, Lieutenant Brown was shot in the throat. One or two of his guns were left behind and taken and another two got stuck in the opening at the stone wall while trying to flee from the advancing Rebels. Under fire, Wright formed his men as best he could and stormed the wall. After a brief struggle, the Confederates broke the Union lines close to where the existing monument to the Fifteenth Massachusetts is standing today, and stormed the guns on the ridge. A group of Yankees advanced, most likely the Sixty-Ninth or Seventy-First New York from General Webb's brigade, toward Wright's left flank where the Forty-Eighth Georgia and the Forty-Eighth Mississippi were fighting desperately to keep the Confederate left flank secure. The musket fire was hot, and lead was flying as men dropped on both sides. Wright turned to see what this new threat was and noted, yet again, that he had no support. To his front, a large force of Confederates followed the Fifteenth Massachusetts and the Eighty-Second New York to the field just north of the Leister House, where the Union troops reformed. Lines were hastily formed by the charging Confederates of the Twenty-Second Georgia and the Second Georgia Battalion. Muskets belched forth death at point-blank range. The edge seemed to be with the Georgia troops when suddenly, on the left and right flank, fire erupted and dozens of men fell as a thick, acrid smoke filled the air. The Rebels broke rank and fell back to the top of Cemetery Ridge. It is at this point that General Wright made his final decision. Since no support had come forward, he decided that he could either charge the Union reinforcements advancing on his beleaguered brigade or retreat and yield the ground and guns that he and his men had fought so hard to gain. The moment came, and Wright called for his men to retreat.

Jack and I believe that the evidence, both historical and paranormal, is overwhelming. Wright most likely claimed the field at the top of Cemetery Ridge, and his troops advanced farther than any other Confederate troops in the three days of fighting. The High Watermark should be a monument to Wright's brigade and the one regiment from Posey's brigade (the Forty-Eighth Mississippi) in the field at the southern base of Cemetery Ridge. Their story was just waiting to be told. Now the ghost soldiers on both sides of the conflict who asked us to tell their story have been honored, and perhaps now they can rest in peace.

Cemetery Hill

ELLIOTT'S
MAP OF THE
BATTLEFIELD OF GETTYSBURG
PENNSYLVANIA

Chapter Twelve

Maniacal Maelstrom of Sound

— By Patrick Burke —

*A*s I stood on the edge of the Brickyard Road, my right foot resting near the Seventh West Virginia left flank marker, I let my mind travel back in time. The summer heat I was experiencing was nothing like the heat on July 2, 1863, which was, reportedly, downright oppressive. I looked over the fields that the Confederate troops of Gen. Richard Ewell's Second Corp traversed in order to get to the bottom of the steep incline on the east side of Cemetery Hill, and I wondered how any of those brave souls could actually have made it through the cannonade and musketry fire.

The Eleventh and Twelfth Corps of the Army of the Potomac sat waiting, entrenched in front of a mass of cannons that bristled out in every direction, like a porcupine's quills, defending all the approaches the Confederates might use to attack the far right flank of the Union line. I imagined the skirmish line—comprised of the Forty-First New York and Thirty-Third Massachusetts—and saw them standing (or in most cases lying down or kneeling on one knee), watching a massive gray line come toward them. I saw a fleeting shadow out in the middle of the field where the Union skirmishers would have been waiting in front of the steep incline to the top of Cemetery Hill. I felt a chill, the kind that only happens when spirit energy is around me. The energy reminded me of a firsthand account from a Union soldier from the Forty-First New York. He reported that suddenly, through the smoke, the Rebels were on them. He fired one shot and chaos ensued around him. "We held the line for about one minute, and then we broke and ran back to the safety of our lines."

The Cemetery Gatehouse on Cemetery Hill, where we captured audio of what sounds like the infamous rebel yell. Courtesy of the Library of Congress.

*Confederate General Richard Ewell, whose troops attacked
the Union entrenchments on Cemetery Hill on July 2, 1863.
Courtesy of the Library of Congress.*

Confederate Col. Isaac Avery of the Sixth North Carolina led his brigade forward as part of the initial advance that day, with Gen. Harry T. Hays's Louisiana Tigers surging on his right. By the time Avery and his troops reached the cover of the bottom of the hill, however, they were already winded. They needed to catch their breath before pushing on to the heights. Huddled at the bottom of the hill, they were perfect targets for Union Col. Leopold von Gilsa's Forty-First New York Infantry, who hid behind makeshift breastworks and rifle pits and fired down into the Confederate ranks.

With sheer determination and in perfect sync, Hays and Avery's brigades charged up the steep slope with bayonets fixed, gave a rebel yell, and smashed into the Union defenders. They overran Von Gilsa's infantry and engaged the cannoneers, who were busy loading and firing cannons. Fierce hand-to-hand combat ensued, with the cannoneers using ramrods and whatever pieces of equipment they could find as weapons. Avery and Hays pressed forward, forcing the Federals from their guns and taking charge of a key strategic position.

I could only imagine what it must have been like for the Union soldiers defending that hill. I had been to this area many times, and almost always I get a quick psi picture, a brief look into the history of the action. When that happens, it isn't difficult for me to step into what a soldier may have been thinking at the time of the action:

> Your cannons open up a brisk and effective fire, you think that should do them, but then you see the line, through brief gaps of the smoke-filled field, closing rank and steadily advancing. Before you know it, an order is given to ready arms and fire. Hot lead is zipping around you, men are falling to the left and right of you, and then that god-awful scream from thousands of throats . . . the rebel yell washes over you and the Confederates smash into your line. It holds for a minute, and then you are racing back to the safety of your entrenched comrades on the slope of Cemetery Hill.

In 1913, veterans of the battle reunited at Gettysburg to reflect and share recollections of the action that took place there fifty years earlier. Courtesy of the Library of Congress.

As a result of heroic fighting by the rebels, the welfare of the entire Army of the Potomac lay in the balance. Confederate Maj. Samuel Tate of the Sixth North Carolina later described the action, "Seventy-five North Carolinians of the Sixth Regiment and twelve Louisianans of Hays's brigade scaled the walls and planted the colors of the Sixth North Carolina and Ninth Louisiana on the guns. It was fully dark. The enemy stood with tenacity never before displayed by them, but with bayonet, clubbed musket, sword, pistols, and rocks from the wall, we cleared the heights and silenced the guns."

But with no support forthcoming, the brave Confederate assault was doomed. While leading his troops forward, Avery fell from his horse bleeding, shot through the neck. Understanding the mortality of his wound, he scribbled a note that he handed to a subordinate. The note simply read, "Tell my father I died with my face to the enemy." Avery died of his wounds the following day. Eventually, the Confederates had to retreat as a result of overwhelming pressure from Union reinforcements. The second day's fighting ended—after much carnage and death—with little ground gained or lost by either side.

Another interesting aspect of the East Cemetery Hill fighting was that it could have been avoided altogether if not for a fateful decision made the day before. On the first day of fighting, the Rebels had pushed the Yankees all the way through Gettysburg to the slight heights overlooking the town. If Confederate Gen. John B. Gordon had roused his brigade, Day Two would have looked a lot different, if in fact fighting was necessary at all. Gen. Richard S. Ewell, Gordon's commander, had instructed him to "take that wooded hill to the west of Cemetery Hill and occupy it." Ewell knew that if the Confederates had seized Culp Hill, the entire Union defenses would have been enfiladed—Rebel cannons would have then raked through the Union line. But Gordon informed Ewell that his brigade had taken the brunt of the attack and were, in his exact words, "done in." This thirty-second exchange may very well have changed the outcome of the battle, and in turn American history. But history doesn't favor hindsight. On that day and forever more, a particular outcome was firmly etched into the fabric of time.

As paranormal investigators, our goal on Cemetery Hill—a century and a half later—was to capture some semblance of the fabled rebel yell. Having sent chills down the spines of many Union soldiers, this unnerving sound has been described in various ways, but the general consensus was that if you heard that yell, you knew that hell on earth was coming. Confederate Col. Keller Anderson of Kentucky's Orphan Brigade described it best when he said, "Then arose that do-or-die expression, that maniacal maelstrom of sound; that penetrating, rasping, shrieking, blood-curdling noise that could be heard for miles and whose volume reached the heavens—such an expression as never yet came from the throats of sane men, but from men whom the seething blast of an imaginary hell would not check while the sound lasted."

With my brother John and friend Mike Hartness accompanying me, we headed to the base of East Cemetery Hill where Avery led the North Carolinians. I turned on my audio recorder and asked the question I had asked 100 times before: "Would you brave men allow me to capture just a bit of what happened here on July 2, 1863 . . . whether it be the rebel yell or the Union huzza, or any other sounds of combat. I would be honored if you gave me a picture, or the rebel yell."

There are times when a paranormal investigator gets what might be considered a special piece of evidence that is more of a personal gift than a random capture. It's a unique moment, when time seems to shift back and allows you to see or hear what happened on that spot years ago. On this day, the brave men who gave their lives for their cause were listening to my request, and, somehow, they made it happen.

When I played back the EVP, I first heard what sounded like a gunshot, and then another, and then a very distinct yell. Shocked that I may have captured the actual rebel yell as an EVP, I compared my audio to a rare recording of the rebel yell at a 1913 reunion of the veterans of the Battle of Gettysburg. In the documentary footage, Confederate veterans are at the Bloody Angle wall—where Confederate Gen. Lewis A. Armistead's brigade temporarily breached the Union line during Pickett's Charge—facing the Union veterans who defended the wall fifty years earlier. Suddenly, you hear one of the Confederate veterans give the rebel yell as he twirled his hat over his head. A Union veteran responds, as if startled, "There it is. That's the rebel yell."

When we compared the EVP to the audio of the old Southern veteran, we noticed that, although the veteran's voice was much older, the cadence and style were almost exactly the same. Was this a residual playback manifested by my thoughts and energy intermingling with the imprinted energies from the battle? Possibly. Or, just maybe it was a ghost soldier who understood that a kindred spirit yearned to hear what had not been heard for a very, very long time.

Triangular Field
Devil's Den

ELLIOTT'S
MAP OF THE
BATTLEFIELD OF GETTYSBURG
PENNSYLVANIA

Made from an accurate Survey of the Ground
by Transit and Chain

Chapter Thirteen

Echoes from the Past

— By Jack Roth —

*A*s we approached the Triangular Field on that cold, damp, misty morning, the only sounds that could be heard were the splatters of gentle raindrops deflecting off the moss-covered rocks and knee-high grass that saturated the landscape. It was six a.m., and the Gettysburg battlefield possessed a mystical quality, even more so than usual.

With heightened caution, we gingerly walked toward a wooden gate that acts as a landmark to where some of the bloodiest fighting took place in July 1863. We didn't want to trip and fall on the soggy ground, so we stepped slowly down a rugged path. We reached a large rock under which we had placed an infrared camera and microphone the night before. They were wet despite the protection of the tarps we left covering them.

"A casualty of field work," I thought, knowing that our technician would be less than pleased about the soaking of his equipment.

I carefully collected everything and handed it off to a fellow field investigator, who promptly took the equipment to the comfort of our heated car. We hoped the rain hadn't destroyed whatever anomalies we may have captured on tape.

Confederate General James Longstreet, who led the Confederate assault on the second day of battle. Courtesy of the Library of Congress.

I lagged behind, savoring the dreamlike atmosphere. I walked back up toward the wooden gate, thinking how great it felt to be on the battlefield without the usual hordes of tourists and busloads of noisy school kids. It was perfectly quiet, almost surreal. As peaceful as this felt, it was hard to believe that hell had once unleashed itself here.

And then I heard them …

The voices emanated from the bottom part of the Triangular Field by its northwest tree line. I initially deduced that I must have been hearing animals. I stopped in my tracks about thirty yards from the car in order to listen more carefully.

Did the wailing battle cries of Confederate infantrymen imprint themselves onto the battleground? Courtesy of the Library of Congress.

"Yip!"

"Hey!"

Silence for a few seconds and then more …

Muddled voices? Men screaming …

… coming up from the tree line toward where the Union line would have been holding ground …

"Yep!"

"Whoop!" "Whoop!"

Cows?

No way—maybe an angry farmer, but not cows.

School kids role-playing on the battlefield?

Not this early, and not in this weather.

I became unnerved.

I waited a few seconds to see if I could distinguish these sounds and pinpoint exactly where they were coming from.

They were getting closer, yet I couldn't see anything. Once more I heard distant screams …

"Yep!" "Yip!"

And then silence.

I waited a few minutes to make sure the sounds had subsided. At this point, my fellow investigator opened the car window and stuck his head out.

"What's up?" he asked. "Did you hear something?"

"Yes. I think I did," I responded. "You're not going to believe this, but I think I just heard rebel yells."

The phantom sounds I heard that morning seemed to originate from the very landscape on which I was standing. Since my strange auditory encounter, I've become fascinated with the Triangular Field, an area of the Gettysburg battlefield that seems to retain a great deal of residual energy. Ringed in by stone walls and woods at the base and up the slope on the right, the field saw a lot of action because Confederate forces had to charge through it in order to take Houck's Ridge and Devil's Den.

There are several historical facts that support what I may have heard on that misty morning. The Triangular Field has become synonymous with the death and destruction associated with the whole of the Battle of Gettysburg. On the morning of the second day of fighting, Confederate Gen. Robert E. Lee believed that if he could simultaneously attack the Union flanks, he could drive the enemy from the field. Part of his plan was to send Gen. James Longstreet's First Army Corps southward to overrun the Union left flank anchored on Little Round Top. In order to even reach Little Round Top, the Confederates had to endure some of the bloodiest fighting of the battle in terrain now referred to as the Triangular Field and Devil's Den. Within just a few hours, thousands would be left either dead or wounded on these blood-soaked grounds.

As confederate brigades under the command of Gen. John Bell Hood made their way southward, they came upon a sloping, triangular field. Waves of Confederate troops from Texas, Arkansas, Alabama, and Georgia crossed this field, clashing with Union regiments from New York, Maine, and Pennsylvania. The Confederate forces were initially cut down by Union artillery posted on top of a small ridge adjacent to the large boulders of Devil's Den, but the Confederates continued to push forward with repeated charges by the Fifteenth Georgia and the First Texas Infantry. Shouting the famous rebel yell, the First Texas charged up the Triangular Field to finally take the summit. The Georgians and Texans proceeded to overrun Devil's Den and took three Union cannons as prizes.

Alexander Hunter, a member of Longstreet's staff, later recalled in his memoirs how the rebel yell would adversely affect the enemy:

> When our reserve, led by Hood's Texas Brigade, the pride and glory of the Army of Northern Virginia, came on a run, gathering up all the fragments of other commands in their front, and this second line clashed straight at the enemy, then I heard the rebel yell with all its appalling significance. I never in my life heard such a fearsome, awful sound … I have often dreamed of it; above the uproar of

a great battle it dominated. On those charging columns of blue it had a decided effect, for it portended capture, mutilation or death and brought eternity very near.

Indeed, the rebel yell was a battle cry used by Confederate soldiers during charges to intimidate the enemy and boost their own morale. Union soldiers, upon hearing the yell from afar, would guess that it was either the Confederates about to attack or rabbits in distress, suggesting a similarity between the sound of the rebel yell and a rabbit's scream. The yell has also been likened to the scream of a wild cat, as well as similar to Native American war cries. One description says it was a cross between an "Indian whoop and wolf-howl." Although nobody has ever actually heard the cries of the fabled banshees from Greek mythology, the rebel yell has often been compared to these blood-curdling wails simply based on their disconcerting effects on those who hear them.

Given the differences in descriptions of the yell, there may have been several distinctive yells associated with the different regiments and their respective geographical areas. Another plausible source of the rebel yell is that it derived from the screams traditionally made by Scottish Highlanders when making a Highland charge during battle. This was a distinctive war cry of the Gael—a high, savage whooping sound.

A great deal of documented eyewitness testimony supports the existence of paranormal activity in the Triangular Field. Confederate sharpshooters have been sighted on the rocks down at the bottom of the field, at the end of the woods, as if preparing to shoot. Strange sounds have been heard, including screams described as rebel yells, emanating from either the wooded area to the right of the wooden gate or down at the bottom end of the field. Artillery blasts have also been heard, as well as the screaming and moaning of wounded and dying soldiers. Union soldiers have been spotted at the left of the gate entrance of the field and have even been known to approach visitors.

Suffice to say, the Triangular Field remains a focal point in our research at Gettysburg. Although perhaps no more haunted than any other part of the battlefield, the smaller, more enclosed nature of the field makes it an ideal place in which to set up a triangulation (no pun intended) of recording equipment, thus making full coverage of the field plausible. In the end, the range and frequency of paranormal activity experienced in this small field cannot be ignored.

Chapter Fourteen

There's the
Devil to Pay

*D*evil's Den is a maze of boulders and rocks that represents one of the most famous landmarks at Gettysburg. On the second day of the battle, this area saw fierce hand-to-hand fighting. Although historians and visitors alike focus mainly on the action in and around the Den, there's a modest elevation located at its northern end known as Houck's Ridge that saw the heaviest fighting of the day. The Confederate juggernaut had to fight through the Triangular Field, over the wall at the top of the field and then up this ridge just in order to first get to the hazardous, jagged-edged ground of Devil's Den.

Capt. James E. Smith's Fourth Battery, New York Light Artillery, consisting of three twenty-pound parrot guns, stationed on the back side of Devil's Den and positioned toward the Triangular Field to aid the 124th New York Volunteer Infantry Regiment, known as the Orange Blossom Boys. The 124th New York was to hold the extreme left flank of the Union defenses on Houck's Ridge. Coming at them were the Fourth and Fifth Texas Brigades of Confederate Gen. John Bell Hood's division with three regiments of Gen. Henry L. Benning's Georgia Brigade in support directly behind them. To make things worse for the Orange Blossom Boys, these particular Confederate soldiers had marched all day and were itching for a fight.

The fighting between the 124th New York and the Texans went back and forth over the top wall three times. The first charge by the New Yorkers ended with the death of their beloved commander, Col. Augustus Van Horne Ellis, who was shot in the forehead and fell dead off his horse. Ironically, on the march to Gettysburg, Ellis prophesied that he would not survive the battle. Maj. James Cromwell rallied the men of the 124th and bravely rode through a storm of bullets in order to retrieve the body of his colonel. According to eyewitness testimony, Cromwell was so gallant that some of the Texans shouted, "Don't shoot at him … don't kill him," but to no avail. He and his gray horse were both shot and killed at the bottom of the field.

The New Yorkers charged a third and final time to retrieve both of their officers' bodies, which they did. However, the Texans gained the wall, and as the Georgians moved up beside them, the Texans jumped up and fired a volley at Smith's Battery, causing horses and men to tumble to the ground. As the Georgians jumped over the wall, Smith was able to save only one of his artillery guns from being captured by the enemy. Eventually, the 124th New York was overrun by fresh Confederate troops, who secured Devil's Den and the southern part of Houck's Ridge. These assaults by Hood's brigades left hundreds of men on both sides killed and more than 1,500 seriously wounded.

Over the years, we've interviewed many eyewitnesses while investigating this area of the battlefield. Once, while filming near Smith's Battery, two women shared a fascinating story with us. Apparently, their husbands were Union reenactors, and they had come to Gettysburg as part of a living-history event during the anniversary of the battle. One evening, the two men (dressed in full reenactment gear) were having a casual conversation while leaning on one of the boulders between Smith's Battery and the 124th New York monuments. As they discussed the day's events, they heard a group of people walking off to their right. When they turned to look, four Union soldiers came into view, their muskets casually slung over their shoulders. They looked tired, drawn, and dusty, and they crossed the road toward the wall at the top of the Triangular Field, which is adjacent to Devil's Den. One of the soldiers looked over, gave them an approving nod with his head, and continued on.

One of the husbands commented that something about those men was odd. He couldn't explain why, but he thought they were out of place. The four soldiers certainly looked the part, but it seemed almost *too* real. He tapped his buddy and said, "Let's go talk to those guys, they really fit the part."

Only a few seconds had passed since they saw the four "reenactors," allowing them plenty of time to catch up to them, but when they reached the wall of Triangular Field, they couldn't find the uniformed men anywhere. In fact, only one other person was there—a man standing at the wall looking into the field. They asked him if he had seen any other reenactors walk by. He replied that he had been standing there for about ten minutes, and they were the first people he had seen since he arrived.

They searched the area in vain and left scratching their heads. What had they just witnessed? The four soldiers looked as solid as the rocks they were leaning on. The eerily authentic condition of their uniforms was certainly impressive, but they were almost too authentic. The tired looks, the dust-covered uniforms, the drawn, almost-sad faces. Did they witness a scene from the past—four Union soldiers walking across Houck's Ridge after the battle had ended? Or maybe it was before the second day's brutality began.

The brief interaction that occurred suggests a genuine spirit encounter. The four soldiers knew the two reenactors were there, and one of them apparently acknowledged that with a nod. This encounter could have been the result of a rip in the fabric of time, a rare moment when the veil between past, present, and future is lifted, leaving those who witness the anomaly with a very strange experience to recount to others. And maybe they were four spirits, bonded in death as they were in life, casualties of one of history's most violent clashes.

Strangely enough, profound stories like this one abound within the reenactor community. Maybe the ghost soldiers see men dressed like them and are drawn to the familiar surroundings they knew while alive. Most reenactors feel a strong connection to the battles and soldiers they honor. Many are descendants whose great-great-great-grandfathers or uncles died in these battles. Others retain vivid and accurate memories as if they were actually participants in these battles, which suggest evidence of possible reincarnation. Whatever the case, reenactors represent ideal witnesses to all types of paranormal activity associated with historic events. In the case of Gettysburg, they are inexplicably drawn to the energy, and many times they offer unique insight regarding the mysterious nature of this most hallowed ground.

Chapter Fifteen

Climbing the Walls

— By Patrick Burke —

At the western end of Devil's Den lies the Triangular Field, into which the phantom soldiers described above seem to have disappeared. The stone wall at the top of this down-sloping field has changed little since local farmers built them in the days before the Civil War. When clearing this Pennsylvania field for crops, they hauled the stones to the side, forming the walls that soldiers later used for protection during the fierce fighting that took place. In retrospect, it did little to lessen the carnage.

On the first day of the Battle of Gettysburg, the Confederates routed Union troops and drove them back through town, but the Federals managed to keep hold of the high ground to the south and east. When the sun rose on the morning of July 2, both were entrenched, but the Army of the Potomac had formed its troops in a hook-like formation that ran from Culp's Hill and Spangler's Spring all the way to Little Round Top. Emboldened by his army's success the previous day, Confederate Gen. Robert E. Lee attached little importance to this topographical disadvantage and launched the Army of Northern Virginia in multiple attacks against the Union flanks.

After a lengthy delay to assemble his forces and avoid detection in his approach march, Lt. Gen. James Longstreet attacked with his First Corps against the Union left flank. As part of this *en echelon* (diagonal) style of attack, a division under the command of Maj. Gen. John Bell Hood was ordered to assault Devil's Den and Little Round Top. In order to accomplish this, General Hood had to first maneuver several of his regiments through the Rose Woods and up the slope of the Triangular Field.

A seasoned soldier who understood that achieving his objective would play a key role in General Lee's efforts to dislodge Union forces, Hood selected some of his best fighting men to lead the attack. At approximately four thirty p.m., the Third Arkansas and the First, Fourth, and Fifth Texas, as well as the Second, Fifteenth, Seventeenth, and Twentieth Georgia, began their advance. When lead elements of the First Texas reached the stone wall, a deadly onslaught of Union artillery and rifle fire awaited. The effect was devastating. Men screamed as each side fired their muskets at point-blank range. As thick smoke filled the air, their breathing and vision became limited. Those who had bayonets stabbed at fleeting shadows; others used their rifles as clubs. Smoke lay on the field like a blanket, but small eddies of air cleared the way for a brief view of the violence that had taken place just moments before.

A soldier who was there recalled the fighting: "Roaring cannons, crashing rifles, screeching shots, bursting shells, hissing bullets, cheers, shouts, shrieks, and groans were the notes of the song of death which greeted the grim reaper, as with mighty sweeps he leveled down the richest field of grain ever garnered on this continent."

As one can only imagine, the Triangular Field is replete with encounters of ghost soldiers still fighting the good fight. Many battlefield visitors have experienced camera malfunctions while trying to take pictures of it. A few years ago, one man took some video footage near a grouping of rocks in the middle of the field. He said he was drawn to the spot and felt overwhelmed with sadness once he got there. When he returned home, he played the videotape and heard a loud, prolonged moan as if a man was writhing in agony. Impossible, he thought, remembering that he was alone in the field when he shot the video.

People have reported seeing Confederate sharpshooters crouched behind the rocks at the bottom of the field. To their utter dismay, some visitors have actually seen impressions in the grass actually moving toward them, and Union soldiers have been sighted and photographed at the gate entrance. Others have heard spectral sounds, including cannon fire, gunshots, screams, moans, and the galloping of horses.

In the fall of 2001, video cameras with infrared capability had just become available, and only a handful of paranormal investigators were using camcorder systems to capture images in the dark. After doing some research on Gettysburg, I decided that the Triangular Field would be an ideal place to shoot some infrared video. On this particular visit, two friends accompanied my family and me to the battlefield for a weekend campout. Both Dennis and Charles had served in the military, and I told them about my theory on capturing historical moments on film. After a nice campfire meal, we left our families and ventured out onto the battlefield.

We started at the Devil's Den parking lot and climbed up through the boulders to the top of Houck's Ridge. I stopped at the Union battery monument, and I could almost feel the sense of apprehension that these artillerymen must have felt as they saw their infantry comrades dying on the field below. As I walked toward the upper wall of the Triangular Field, I turned on my camcorder and began to film. I asked permission of any spirits present to capture their images on my camcorder—or to at least record what the battle sounded like. When I got to the wall, Dennis proceeded to climb over and lean on it. Charles stood just behind my left shoulder as I called out for the boys to come forth and join us.

Within seconds, a series of energy signatures sped across my LED screen. I told Dennis and Charles to head into the field while I filmed from behind the wall. As Charles moved over the wall, I saw a man dressed in a white shirt and black pants walking about halfway up the slope of the field toward the wall. At this point, my senses were at full alert, as the energy in the field was intense, and I knew something was going to happen.

As I filmed the man walking, I saw a movement behind him and suddenly felt a rush of wind go by me. I refocused on the area to his left where Dennis and Charles had gone to sit down. Feeling drawn to that side of the field, I looked to my right and filmed along the wall. I swept the field briefly with the camera but had an overwhelming urge to film to my right again. I turned and saw the man from earlier getting closer to the wall, so I steadied the camera on him. As I focused, I heard a little voice in my head say, "Hold steady. You're not going to want to miss this!" So I fixed the camcorder on him until the feeling dissipated about a minute later.

While reviewing the footage later that night, we knew immediately that we had captured something extremely rare: a full-bodied, detailed apparition moving on video. In the playback, as the real man walks toward the wall, another individual—semitransparent and in Civil War uniform—manifests in front of him, running frantically toward the wall. Without slowing down, he jerks his leg up and over as if trying to jump it…an astounding visual to say the least. Stunned, Dennis and Charles asked me what in the world I had just taped. Trying to be as logical and objective as possible, I concluded that we may have just documented one of two things: 1) a residual haunting in which we captured the playback of a soldier actually running toward the wall during the battle; or 2) the spirit of a soldier who honored my request to show us what the battle must have been like that day.

*These three video captures show a ghost soldier
crossing over the stone wall in the Triangular Field
in front of an investigator. Photos by Patrick Burke.*

In either case, this video footage remains one of the most profound and compelling pieces of evidence we've ever captured. The implications are staggering. When analyzed objectively, it leaves little wiggle room for debunkers. There, in plain view for everyone to see, is a full-bodied apparition whose appearance and actions tie in directly to the location in which the video was shot—a Civil War soldier running for his life. The only thing the video doesn't convey is the horror that this poor young man must have been feeling.

But how could my video camera capture something I didn't see while shooting it? Many contemporary paranormal researchers believe that ghosts exist as some form of electromagnetic energy, and science dictates that all energy is traceable in the light spectrum. When I first decided to investigate battlefields, I wanted to prove beyond a shadow of a doubt that lost souls still roamed the places where they died tragically. I could attempt to capture ghostly images by using an ultraviolet filter on my 35mm camera, but that would only work in the daylight and I would only be capturing a still image. Ideally, I wanted to capture an apparition in movement, and to do that I needed a camcorder.

Although there's no official manual that describes how to use a camcorder to capture ghosts, I believe that you *can* increase your chances of success. As a sensitive, I use my intuition when attempting to record the past and listen to that little voice inside my head that always leads me down the right path. We all have it; some of us just listen more intently to it than others. By quieting the mind, I've learned how to gather information from both residual imprints and direct telepathic communication with discarnate spirits. This method can be applied to obtaining video evidence by allowing yourself to be immersed in the energies that surround you—or, as some would say, tuning into the frequencies associated with paranormal activity.

I've found that the best way to connect to other realms is to slowly ramp up your skill through measured exercises. As the old adage goes, practice makes perfect! For example, find a comfortable chair that allows you to sit with your back straight and your feet firmly on the floor. Close your eyes and take a deep breath through your nose for a long count of four, expanding your diaphragm to the maximum. Next, breathe out to a count of three. Repeat this three or four times as you attempt to clear your head of all thoughts and quiet the noise in your mind. Once you've achieved this, count to ten. Remember, the only thing that you should be focused on is the current number—nothing else. For example, if you think to yourself as you're focusing on the number three, "Wow, this is easy," or "What should I make for dinner tonight," you failed to be fully focused and need to start over again.

How can this simple exercise help you to capture paranormal evidence on a battlefield? Communicating with the spirits of those who have passed on requires an enormous amount of focus, and these mental exercises will help you with that. If you can tune in to the energies around you, you'll be able to locate those areas that are more likely to "host" a paranormal event. Therefore, you'll have a better chance of capturing historical moments with whatever equipment you might be using. Clearing the mind is the first step to being able to feel the spirit energies around us. And remember, always ask permission to interact with them (or capture their image or voice) so that you can share their stories with others and keep their memories alive.

Chapter Sixteen

The Gift

— By Patrick Burke —

It was a cool and pleasant August evening in 2007 when Darryl "Smitty" Smith, Michael Hartness, and I decided to visit our old ghost soldier buddies at the Triangular Field. Mike, unlike many of us on the American Battlefield Ghost Hunter's Society (ABGHS) team, had never experienced anything out of the ordinary at this location, but his luck was about to change.

Mike desperately wanted to have a firsthand paranormal encounter, and knowing what kind of compelling evidence the team had captured in the Triangular Field on past visits made him even more anxious to experience something. The Triangular Field offers as good an opportunity to have a paranormal encounter as any other place in Gettysburg, as unsuspecting visitors have reported many strange accounts over the years. This makes perfect sense, as some of the most vicious fighting of the Civil War took place in this small field between Devil's Den and the Wheatfield during the second day of the battle. The Confederate forces had to first assault and wrest the Wheatfield away from the Union troops. Then, once this area was cleared and secured, the Confederate troops could move on the Triangular Field and then assault their primary object, the Devil's Den.

As we approached the stone wall at the top of the field, I decided to stir up whatever paranormal energies I could. "Hey, boys!" I yelled out into the field. "We're back, and it sure would be great if y'all would honor us with a bit of what happened here on July 2, 1863. I know Mike would surely appreciate it."

Smitty moved over to the gate at the upper wall and proceeded to film that area of the field. Mike and I walked down to the middle of the field, near the right side of the wall as you walk down toward the bottom. The Triangular Field is normally quite active with visitors and ghost hunters, but on this particular day very few people were present. I walked down the sloped field approximately twenty paces apart from Mike and turned my camcorder toward the undergrowth, some of which stood more than six feet tall. Due to the height of the grass, I couldn't see into the wooded area where the Third Arkansas and First Texas charged Houck's Ridge during the battle.

Suddenly there was a rush of air, and we heard what sounded like hundreds of people moving in the woods. We both looked at each other at the same time and asked simultaneously, "Do you hear that!"

The noise got louder as this "attacking force" appeared to get closer to us. The air around us suddenly pulsated as if it had taken on a life of its own. I knew immediately that Mike and I had stepped fully into a paranormal moment, one of those rare moments when the very fabric of time "rips open" and reveals—albeit briefly—what happened long ago. Every one of our senses was heightened, and we could actually distinguish all the sounds associated with a mass of moving soldiers—rifle butts smacking low branches, canteens slapping hips, and the tramp of thousands of feet on dry leaves and twigs. I ran up the hill as Mike came toward me. We found a break in the grass, and as we turned down this path we were surrounded by the sound of men running. I could hear the sounds of labored breathing and muttering voices when a sudden flash in my mind's eye showed a glimpse of the men before me. With our hearts beating faster than you could ever imagine, we ran toward the wall. I held the camcorder over my head, pointing it toward the woods in the hopes of catching something through the grass. When I reached the wall, I brought the camera back down. Finally, I thought to myself, I might be able to capture the actual historical battle on film. I seriously believed that elusive moment might actually be at hand.

And then, a woman with a small group of people behind us shouted, "Hey! You find anything!"

At that moment the paranormal event stopped, and the regular night noises returned to the environment. Mike and I looked at each other and laughed. We realized we had just been graced with the ability to view living history from those who actually participated in it—getting a glimpse of actual historic events as they occurred almost a century and a half earlier. At times like this, one is often speechless. We smiled at the woman and answered, "Nah, nothing here."

We asked for a personal experience, and we truly believe our buddies on the other side heard us and gave us an astounding gift. Whenever I have an experience like this on a battlefield, I feel extremely humbled. The fact that these brave souls feel connected enough with me to actually allow me to witness history as it really happened is just incredible, and I'm truly grateful for it.

The Valley of Death

Chapter Seventeen

High, Low, and Pretty Much All Over

— By Jack Roth —

Plum Run Creek, also known as Bloody Run, is a small stream that runs through a gorge known as the Valley of Death. This valley is located between Devil's Den and Little Round Top, which made it a natural clashing point during the Battle of Gettysburg. The creek earned its infamous nickname after it ran red with the blood of fallen soldiers, mostly Confederates who were trying to overrun Little Round Top. On July 4, 1863, one day after the battle ended, heavy rains caused the creek's shallow banks to overflow, and several Confederate wounded, who couldn't move and had not yet been retrieved by their comrades, tragically drowned. Veterans of the battle described the valley surrounding Plum Run as littered with so many bodies that it took over a week after the battle ended for all of the fallen men to be buried.

It all started at approximately five p.m. on July 2, 1863, when Union Brig. Gen. Samuel W. Crawford moved two of his Pennsylvania infantry brigades forward across the Valley of Death (which subsequently garnered the nickname the Slaughter Pen) against approaching Confederate infantry who were attempting to reach the summit of Little Round Top and flank the Union left. Between the Second U.S. Sharpshooters, who were stationed behind an insulating stone wall at the base of the hill and Union Capt. James Smith's remaining cannons from his Fourth New York Battery, severe casualties were inflicted on Rebel infantry from both the Second Georgia regiment advancing along the creek, and the Fourth and Fifth Texas and Fifteenth Alabama regiments advancing toward the open south side of Little Round Top. The Valley of Death and Plum Run Creek became an inferno of gun and cannon fire, resulting in high casualties and forever entrenching these geographic landmarks into the tragic lore of the battlefield.

Early one evening in the spring of 2004, while investigating Devil's Den, a young couple in our group looked out of their car and saw what they described as bright flashes of light appearing randomly above the tree line just beyond Plum Run Creek. Most orb-like phenomena tend to be photographic in nature and are very controversial, but the fact that they saw these lights with the naked eye makes this a more unique encounter. It was a very clear night, and they were able to watch these flashes of light for approximately three minutes as they appeared to move lower and closer to them as time went by. As is often the case when witnesses have the time to carefully analyze what they are seeing, they were able to rule out some mundane possibilities. They stand by their testimony and remain adamant that these lights were not car or plane lights, flashlight reflections, shooting stars, or fireflies (aka lightning bugs).

I immediately documented their description of the lights, and we stayed around Plum Run Creek for a while in case the lights came back. The lights did not return, but the witnesses managed to take digital photographs while observing them, and as a result captured glowing anomalies on just about every one of their shots. No details could be discerned from the photographs, but they did confirm the validity and location of the sighting. The following is their testimony:

"It was probably around nine thirty p.m., around that time frame, and we were over by Devil's Den, parked down farther to the right of the last few spots if you were looking down at the parking lot from the big boulders," said Eric. "Almost everyone from our group was back on the other side of the parking lot heading over toward Little Round Top. There was also a bunch of other people who were walking up toward the top of Devil's Den ... moving up the hill with flashlights. We decided to stay down more toward the woods near the creek because it was much quieter down there."

Tammy added that they also got back into the car because they were cold.

Dead Confederate soldiers in the Slaughter Pen. Courtesy of the Library of Congress.

Eric continued: "We were just kind of hanging out, and it was pretty dark over in that spot and we started noticing some flashes of light kind of up high over the tops of the trees."

I asked them what they thought these lights may have been at first, and it occurred to Eric right away that there could be a road back behind the wooded area and that they could be seeing car lights flashing through the trees as the cars drove by, but they ruled this out and then thought maybe it was a low-flying plane, and that they were seeing its lights blinking as it flew behind the trees.

"But that just wasn't right; it didn't fit the description because a plane never came into view, and the lights didn't flash in a line," said Eric. "They were random in nature, and they covered a pretty wide area above the trees. At first they were up high. Right after we ruled out car or plane lights, we started seeing more flashes down low, and much closer to us."

"They were high, low, and pretty much all over, which was just very strange because they didn't seem to look like any lights we had ever seen," added Tammy. "They were more like starbursts than anything else."

"Could they have been the flashlights from the other people who were climbing up the rocks at Devil's Den?" I asked.

"No way," Tammy quickly responded. "These lights were way too bright, and they didn't move like someone was moving a flashlight around. I can say with certainty they weren't flashlights."

"Right," added Eric, "and they were all over, so we were able to rule out the plane theory and the flashlight theory right away. Then the last thing that occurred to us was that they might be lightning bugs, you know, fireflies, but again it wasn't a good explanation. These lights were much brighter and bursting."

"So they weren't really floating around like fireflies do," I said.

"They weren't pulsating as much as they were flashing," said Eric. "In other words, there was no dimming up and down, just very quick flashes. You couldn't see any kind of pulse like you would see from a lightning bug.

And right about the time we ruled out just about everything 'normal' it could be, they started really flashing all around us."

I asked Tammy how she felt at this point, and she said she started to get very intrigued because the lights were moving closer to them. She wasn't scared at all, but very excited.

"Tammy jumped out of the car with the digital camera and started snapping a few photographs, and from what we could tell right at first glance, there are some round circular lights that showed up in them," said Eric.

Tammy showed me her digital camera, and these lights appeared every picture she took. Some seemed farther away then others, but a few were really close to them.

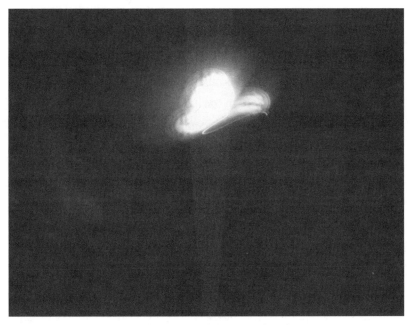

Photo of one of the strange light anomalies that Tammy
and Eric saw that night. Photo courtesy of Jack Roth.

"It was so cool," said Tammy, "because your intuition just tells you these things were not natural. They seemed other-worldly."

Eric reminded me that it was their first paranormal investigation, and it was the first time they had ever experienced anything like that.

"It was very fun, very cool," he added.

Tammy, thinking it might be time-of-day related, wanted to come back at the same time the next night to see if they could see the same thing.

A great idea, I told them that we would definitely make it a point of doing that.

I also expressed my excitement over the fact that their first paranormal experience was such a positive one.

"Did you feel strange while you watched these lights, or did you feel like the atmosphere around you changed at all?" I asked.

"We were in the car at first, but the windows were open, and then of course we got out to take pictures as the lights got closer. But it's funny you ask that, because as time went by, it seemed as if everything else around us didn't exist," said Eric. "I can't recall any sounds, natural or man-made, so maybe I was just very focused on the lights. I can't speak for Tammy."

"I ask this because sometimes people experience what is known as the Oz Factor, which is when the environment actually changes as you're experiencing a paranormal event," I explained. "The atmosphere becomes different to people, and it's very hard to explain."

"I felt strange, but Eric and I were talking to each other, so that interaction was real," said Tammy. "The lights themselves were strange, though. They seemed not of this world, so to speak. I think you can just tell when something isn't right."

We hung out for a while longer to see if anything else manifested, but all was quiet. Eric wanted to know what happened in this area of the battlefield that might explain the lights. I told him that soldiers were fighting all throughout this area and many of them died in this creek. There was a lot of gun and cannon fire, which could explain the lights as a residual phenomenon. "Many people see flashes of light all over the battlefield, and they aren't all fireflies," I assured them. "It makes sense," I said, "but only if you believe residual hauntings are possible."

"I can see that for sure," said Tammy.

"They did look like flashes of gunfire in the dark," said Eric. "That would be the most accurate description yet. Wow. I can really see that, but why high above the trees at first?"

"I can't say for sure, but certain kinds of artillery fire did explode above the trees, raining down shrapnel over the enemy," I explained. "We can never know for sure, but I think your experience tonight was a really good one."

I still think about Tammy and Eric's experience for several reasons. First and foremost, they were really cool people and made for outstanding eyewitnesses. They weren't flaky and really performed an objective analysis regarding what they saw *as* they saw it, which should be commended. Also, my intuition tells me they saw something truly paranormal. Usually, lights and orbs represent tenuous evidence at best, but when they are seen by more than one witness for a prolonged period of time with the naked eye and appear in a way that defies all logical explanations, then such an event should be taken seriously and documented thoroughly.

The location factor also comes into play in this instance. Bloody Run, the Slaughter Pen, Devil's Den—these places are bathed in a history of bloodshed, emotional trauma, and loss of life, all of which must be taken into account when examining evidence or eyewitness testimony, especially when such evidence imitates the natural phenomena associated with the actual battle (gun flashes, cannon fire bursts, etc.).

For me, the best part of this story remains the fact that Tammy and Eric had what they truly believed was a real paranormal experience, and it was a positive and exciting one. We will probably never know what they saw that night, but I remain very happy for them because they experienced something special. Experiences like theirs often urge people to become more involved in paranormal research. I sincerely hope they continue to show an interest in investigating paranormal phenomena and approaching it in such an objective, logical manner. I, for one, believe they would make great field researchers.

Little Round Top

Chapter Eighteen

Fight or Flight

*J*ust behind the Peach Orchard lies the Trostle Farm, one of the areas where Confederate Gen. James Longstreet's forces clashed with Union Gen. Daniel Sickles's Third Corps on the second day of the battle. The fighting in this area was vicious, and it was the result of a bold salient—a maneuver that projects into the position of the enemy—made by Sickles that almost jeopardized the entire Union army. Sickles—a controversial, flamboyant, and charismatic officer—didn't like the unfavorable nature of his original position on Cemetery Ridge and decided to move his troops forward toward the Peach Orchard to meet the enemy head-on. Not only did Sickles disobey Maj. Gen. George Gordon Meade's direct order to hold his ground, Sickles exposed both sides of the Third Corps to enfilading fire and overextended the Union line.

As Sickles directed his forces in front of the Trostle Farm on a slight rise in the landscape, he could see the battle developing, but before he could meet the incoming Rebels, he was struck in the right leg by shrapnel. Being an old warhorse, Sickles told his aides to place a tourniquet on his leg and continued to direct his troops for several more minutes before being carried off the field. His leg was later amputated; a result that many officers believed saved him from being court-martialed for his rash and perilous action.

*Confederate dead in the Peach Orchard, where heavy fighting occurred
on the second day of the battle. Courtesy of the Library of Congress.*

As the Confederate juggernaut pressed forward and Sickles's troops
began to crumble, Union forces continued to rush men in to fill the gaps
in their lines. The fighting around Trostle Farm was intense, and many
visitors to the battlefield have reported paranormal activity in that area.
On a July night in 2006, a group of us made plans to meet at Gettysburg
for an investigation. Ed Dubil Jr. (Little Ed) and his dad (Big Ed) wanted
to do some ghost hunting around Trostle Farm and the Peach Orchard,
so we met there. We were all happy to have Brutus, Little Ed's ghost hunting dog, with us. This was the first time I had the chance to work with
Brutus, and it turned out to be an incredible experience.

Union General Daniel Sickles, who disobeyed orders and exposed the Union Third Corps to a battering of enemy fire. Courtesy of the Library of Congress.

As a sensitive, I usually get a feel for the presence of ghost soldiers before most other people. My brother John and Big Ed were at the front and to the left of the barn as you face it from the Peach Orchard. Along the shoulder of the road, they set up two tripods with Sony "night-shot" camcorders as they talked about the various places they had investigated. Little Ed, Brutus, and two close friends of mine, Chris Carouthers (a talented sensitive) and Karen Mitchell-Carouthers (a rocket scientist...seriously!) joined me on the backside of the barn, standing near the area where wounded soldiers were cared for during and after the battle.

Little Ed and I were talking about some of the experiences he had with Brutus and his father on the battlefield, and he recounted this story for me:

We were at the Eleventh Pennsylvania Infantry monument on Oaks Hill. The Eleventh had a mascot, a dog named Sally. Dad and I had been there before and never got any evidence, but on this over-cast morning we decided to make another visit. Brutus did what all dogs do, checked out the area and then lay down near the statue of Sally. Dad wandered off videotaping while I began taking ran-dom pictures with my camera and turned on my digital recorder, placing it on the monument near the statue of Sally. No one else was there, just Dad, Brutus, and me. As I normally do when on the battle-field, I thought about what it must have been like during the fighting, and also about the men who survived and went back to search, not only for their fallen comrades, but for Sally too. She had been miss-ing since they retreated on July 1st. I imagined the relief they must have felt when they saw Sally, looking a bit sickly but alive, guarding their dead comrades. Suddenly Brutus sat up, his ears perked and his breathing very still, and then he trotted over to me. Later that night as Dad and I were going through the photos and videos, I played the recorder, and all was quiet. All you could hear was my camera taking a few shots, that is, until we heard a whistle and a man's voice calling out, "Here boy!"

As we walked toward the paved road that cuts through the Peach Orchard and past the barn, we could see John and Big Ed about 175 feet away, near their stationary cameras. I felt a sense of urgency as I watched Brutus stop, raise his ears and seem to hold his breath. I asked Little Ed what Brutus was doing, and his response was, "It's called fight or flight. He is deciding if what he hears is a threat and, if so, can he win." Little Ed squatted down behind Brutus and took a photo between the dog's ears. The photograph revealed an orb about a foot away from where Brutus was standing.

As we walked around the barn to the spot where Sickles lost his leg, Chris (the sensitive) began to feel nauseated and confused. There was definitely a sense of dread around us, which I associated with the Union soldiers as they struggled to hold their position against overwhelming odds.

And then, suddenly, I heard the rebel yell. All around me it seemed like men were running, "Dear God," I thought. "This is how it felt to be on the receiving end of that howl!" Brutus's ears were up and his body was tense. Chris, Karen, and Little Ed had moved about fifty feet away from me, and they showed no signs of hearing anything at all . . . and then the moment was gone.

A few days later my brother John called me and said he believed he had captured a mass of men rushing past the barn toward the Peach Orchard. When we reviewed the footage together, we could see (although the quality of the video is lacking) a mass of shadows crossing between the fence rails and the barn, and we could even see the shadow of a flag waving. Brutus, who has since passed away, was able to experience this paranormal activity before any of us became aware of anything out of the ordinary. Like most animals, he had a keen sense of such things. Brutus was a great field investigator in his own right, and he will be missed.

Chapter Nineteen

Chaos and Carnage

— By Jack Roth —

*O*n the afternoon of July 2, 1863, a twenty-acre field of wheat on the John Rose farm became the stage for some of the most vicious and costly fighting associated with not only the Battle of Gettysburg, but of the entire Civil War. Although golden wheat grew tall on hundreds of other fields across southern Pennsylvania around the time of the battle, this patch of land would forever become known as the "Bloody Wheatfield," somehow relegating all other wheat fields to secondary status.

In the summer of 1863, the Wheatfield was surrounded by wood lots owned by the John Rose family. A small road and a large patch of land known as Trostle's Woods snaked its northern border. A worm-rail fence bordered its western edge, separating it from Rose Woods and a rocky knoll known as the Stony Hill, which overlooked the Valley of Death before the Little Round Top. A stone wall separated the field from the section of Rose's Woods that stretched along its southern edge. Immediately to the east of the field was Houck's Ridge and Devil's Den, and beyond that was Little Round Top, the ultimate prize for the Confederates because the entire Union artillery reserves and supplies trains were parked just on the other side. With that in mind, Confederate forces attacked the Union defenses like a series of tidal waves on the second day of fighting.

Confederate dead at the edge of the Rose Woods, where Southern forces emerged and collided with Union brigades in the Wheatfield. Courtesy of the Library of Congress.

Positioned at a relatively secure location on Cemetery Ridge on the morning of July 2, General Sickles believed he saw higher ground ahead of him and advanced his entire Corp without orders, exposing the Union's left flank. His lines now stretched through fields far in front of those chosen by the Union's commanding general, George Gordon Meade. One such area along this new line was the now-infamous twenty-acre field of wheat.

In the late afternoon, Confederate forces began their coordinated assault against Union lines beginning at its southernmost point at Devil's Den and Little Round Top. As Southern brigades advanced in the direction of the Wheatfield, they were completely unaware that Union Gen. Daniel E. Sickles, the commander of the Army of the Potomac's Third Corps, had advanced his men to this location. In fact, the fighting in both the Wheatfield and the Peach Orchard actually occurred by accident—the result of Sickles ill-advised and unauthorized tactical maneuver (see chapter 18: Fight or Flight).

At four thirty p.m., when Confederate Gen. George T. Anderson's Brigade of Georgians and the Third Arkansas emerged from the Rose Woods and collided with Union brigades from the Third Corps in the Wheatfield, a melee of epic proportions began. Chaos ensued with a series of confusing attacks and counterattacks by eleven brigades from both sides, resulting in heavy casualties. In what must have seemed like utter pandemonium for the soldiers involved, the field changed hands six times in two hours.

A dead Union soldier in the Wheatfield, where Union forces suffered more than 3,000 casualties and the Confederates incurred almost 1,500 casualties during the three-hour melee. Courtesy of the Library of Congress.

By seven thirty p.m., the battle of the Wheatfield was over. The wheat lay trampled and the ground left soaked in blood with the dead and wounded stacked three and four deep. The casualty rates appalled even the most hardened of commanders. The Sixty-First New York lost 60 percent of its number, all killed and wounded. The Fifty-Third Pennsylvania lost 59 percent. The Seventeenth U.S. lost 58 percent. The Union regiments averaged losses of approximately one-third, with the Confederate regiments averaging about the same. In total, the Union suffered casualties of 3,215 and the Confederates 1,394. More than 4,000 men were killed or wounded in just over two hours of fighting. Some of the wounded managed to crawl to Plum Run but couldn't cross it. The river ran red with their blood, earning it the nickname "Bloody Run."

A New York soldier described the aftermath of the day's carnage: "Silence followed the roar and tumult of battle. Through the darkness the rifles of the distant pickets flashed like fireflies, while, nearer by, the night air was burdened with the plaintive moans of wounded men who were lying between the lines and begging for water."

As one might expect, the Wheatfield represents a great location in which to conduct paranormal research. On May 8, 2004, our investigative team conducted a daytime experiment designed to cover the entire twenty-acre field. We performed a grid-like walkthrough with several participants. The "sweepers" spread out approximately fifteen yards apart and began walking across the field in unison from southern to northern edge. They each possessed handheld equipment in the form of still and/or video cameras, voice recorders, ion detectors, and EMF meters. Simultaneously, we set up video cameras along the higher elevations in order to capture various bird's-eye views of the entire field.

I monitored the walkthrough with a walkie-talkie from the southern edge of the field while Jon, a fellow investigator, monitored the experiment with another walkie-talkie from the northern edge. We did this so each sweeper could make at least one of us aware of an anomalous event, and we could then coordinate the movements of the entire team to the point of interest. Once they all reached the northern edge of the field, Jon would send them back through for a reverse walkthrough.

It was a beautiful day with temperatures in the mid-70s, low humidity, and partly cloudy skies. Within seconds of beginning the experiment, a participant named Todd yelled aloud in excitement that he saw something. We rushed over to where he was standing.

"I guess there were six or seven of us crossing the field," he said. "I was the first person from the western edge tree line and probably fifteen yards from the edge. I was about forty yards into it when from my right-hand side I saw a light traveling to the left toward the tree line."

"Can you describe it?" I asked.

"I didn't see or sense anything but I saw a light, just a pure white light that was three or maybe four feet long and approximately eight to ten inches in diameter," explained Todd. "I deal a lot with animals and I know it definitely wasn't any kind of animal. It was about a foot and a half off the ground and a bit higher than the grass, and it was traveling from right to left toward the tree line. I was on the left hand side, and when I saw it I didn't have time to take a picture because it was moving so fast."

"Did it move in a straight line?" I asked.

"No," he continued. "It went and circled around a large rock in a collection of rocks that were in the tree line and then it was just gone. It was really quick, instantaneous—and it definitely wasn't an animal."

I continued the questioning. "Have you ever seen anything like it before, or was it completely unique to you?"

"I can't explain what it was," he said. "This is the first time I've ever seen anything like this. It was definitely there, and it was a light about three or four feet long and eight to ten inches wide. It seemed to just come out of the grass at a point west of my line. I thought it was being disturbed in some way as we all walked closer to it, and it disappeared into the tree line, moving out of the field very quickly."

He added that it was very clear and extremely bright. It was also very fast as it shot into the woods.

"Could it have been a reflection of something hitting the sunlight?" I wondered.

"This was a solid, bright, white light," Todd reassured me. "It wasn't a bird or any animal I've ever seen before. It was luminescent, too big to be a bug and too fast to be a bird. I wouldn't have yelled out if it didn't register as something really out of the ordinary."

Considering what Todd just witnessed, we decided to focus our efforts on the wooded area on the western edge of the field where he witnessed the light vanish. We took readings and photographs along the edge of the tree line and slowly made our way into the woods. After only a few minutes, another participant, Rebecca, approached Jon and me with a look of horror on her face. She was pale and literally shaking, and we attempted to calm her down. Once she reached a decent state of calm, I asked her to describe what happened.

"We were all walking around looking for the light Todd saw," she said. "I went off to the right toward the very edge of the woods and climbed up those rocks and stepped over that fallen tree to the right. I was just standing very still at that point trying to get an electromagnetic reading. I looked up, and about eye level with me or maybe a little above I saw a face. It was very solid and very clear. It was a man's face. He had dark hair, very heavy thick hair, full facial hair that was very dark, black almost, and then he locked eyes with me."

"Where was he exactly?" I asked.

"He was by that tree, but just his face," Rebecca pointed to a tree on the edge of the Wheatfield. "I couldn't see a body. He had the kind of facial hair that was very common during the Civil War. And his face looked dirty."

"Did he have a hat?" I asked.

"No," she said, still shaken by her experience, "not that I could see."

I asked her what she did when she first saw the face.

"This is the first time I ever saw anything like this," she said. "The last thing I thought of was grabbing my camera. I just stared back at him trying to decide if I was really seeing what I thought I was seeing, and when I could finally breathe again, I tried to motion for someone without speaking, you know, like 'Come here!' because I didn't want to look away from him yet. But nobody saw my gestures. I locked eyes with this guy for what seemed like an eternity, and I finally looked over and everybody was gone.

"When I looked back, he was gone. I actually stayed there looking for some more to see if it could've been a shadow or a configuration of shadows, or something that I could've mistaken, but I never found it again."

"It's great that you stayed and didn't run away," I said. "Was he threatening?"

"It was very definitely a man, and he was very mean," she explained. "It was *not* a pleasant experience, and it scared the heck out of me because he was very, very hostile. I just couldn't breathe when it happened. I just couldn't even breathe and you know when you feel tingly all over? Well that's how I felt. It was a very negative experience. He was just mean-spirited."

I assured Rebecca that he was gone now and she was safe with us.

Debbie, another participant in the experiment, told us that she took a photograph of the tree line around the same time Rebecca had her experience because she sensed something by that tree. We checked Debbie's photo and were amazed to see a white, glowing orb about the size of a large grapefruit or a small soccer ball to the left of the tree. It was located in the same area of the woods where Todd saw the glowing object enter the tree line and about twenty yards south of where Rebecca saw the man's face.

Debbie's photo was taken during the day in good lighting conditions, which rules out the often-misidentified dust particles that tend to illuminate when digital shots are taken in low-light conditions (which they usually are) and the flash goes off. The unique natures of the photo stems from the fact that such clear and pronounced glowing orb manifestations captured in daylight hours are quite rare. Let's not forget that Debbie also sensed something by the tree, which prompted her to take the photo in the first place. Therefore, her psychic intuition becomes a corroborative factor in this instance.

We also examined the area where Rebecca saw the face and saw nothing in the environment that could have resembled what she described. We did this in order to rule out pareidolia or matrixing, which is the phenomenon of seeing a familiar shape or form in random combinations of shadows and light. The shape or form itself is called simulacrum. One of the primary functions of the human mind is to make order out of chaos. Therefore, we have a tendency to see what looks like a face or familiar form in jagged rocks, dirt, water, clouds, and even flames. The outdoor environment in Gettysburg is lush with trees, bushes, rocks, water sources, and foliage in various stages of decomposition—combinations of shapes and forms that often can be mistaken for soldiers, horses, guns, and other elements associated with the battle.

What is extremely compelling about this series of incidents in the Wheatfield is the fact that three witnesses experienced profound phenomena, within minutes of each other, all of which can be linked in a logical manner. Let's recap: The first person (Todd) sees a visual sighting of an orb-like object streaking across the Wheatfield; the second person (Rebecca) experiences a harrowing apparitional sighting of a man's face in the same area where the orb-like object is last seen; and the third person (Debbie) senses something and takes a photograph of a similar orb-like object · in the exact location where the first streak of light apparently enters the woods.

This daylight orb was captured by the tree line minutes
after being seen in the Wheatfield. Photo by Debbie Estep.

In the world of paranormal field research, this is known as a "big deal." When it comes to mostly nontangible and nonreplicable phenomena such as ghosts, science refuses to even consider their validity. Corroborative evidence represents the best validation of the phenomena we currently have at our disposal.

Could these anomalies be associated with the energies of one or more of the thousands of souls who lost their lives in the Wheatfield during the most epic battle of the war? We may never know for certain, but when solid eyewitness accounts of ghostly phenomena are encountered in an area where extreme emotional trauma took place in such a short period of time, it makes further study in and around the Wheatfield worthy of our time and effort.

Chapter Twenty

The Eternal Battle

— By Jack Roth —

Nestled on the crest of the southern slope of Little Round Top, the patch of ground where Union Col. Joshua Lawrence Chamberlain and the Twentieth Maine repulsed Confederate attempts to collapse the Union left flank appears inconspicuous enough. In fact, when we attempted to find this location during our first-ever visit to the battlefield, we struggled to find it. Once we did, paranormal activity began in earnest before we could even unpack any of our equipment.

We arrived at the battlefield on a beautiful fall afternoon, drove around and eventually headed toward the two rocky hills that marked the locations of Little Round Top and Big Round Top. Winding roads lined with memorials guided us around the Valley of Death and Devil's Den, and finally to the base of Little Round Top.

As we drove, we felt overwhelmed by the significance of the location. We were in Gettysburg, where for three days in 1863 some of the most vicious and costly fighting ever experienced by armies took place on American soil; where more than 51,000 casualties accumulated like snowflakes during a winter storm as armed men fought to the death over political and moral issues that many of them didn't bother to comprehend. The events that played out on this patch of land signified the turning point of the Civil War, which on a larger scale was a critical turning point in the history of our young nation. Before 9/11, everything we knew about this country could be categorized in terms of "before the Civil War" and "after the Civil War." We were in arguably the most significant place in U.S. history, where tens of thousands of young men experienced the hellish and indescribable nature of warfare.

Dead soldiers from both armies were strewn all over
Little Round Top. Courtesy of the Library of Congress.

The summit of Little Round Top—like the rest of the battlefield—is strewn with monuments dedicated to various individuals, companies, regiments, and corps. The fighting on and around Little Round Top on July 2, 1863, was both intense and strategically critical. Union Gen. Strong Vincent's brigade held off wave after relentless wave of Confederate assaults as a number of Alabama and Texas regiments from Maj. Gen. John Bell Hood's division attempted to flank the Army of the Potomac. Chamberlain's Twentieth Maine successfully defended the end of the Union line on the southern slope (the extreme left), with the engagement culminating in a dramatic downhill bayonet charge that essentially ended the Southern advance.

The significance of this action cannot be overstated: If Chamberlain and his men had faltered that day, Southern forces would have flanked the Union left and crushed the Federal army in a rout. Instead, the failure to break the Union's defensive line forced General Lee into attempting an ill-advised assault (Pickett's Charge, see chapter 22) on the Union center the following day, which led to a devastating Southern defeat and the end of the Battle of Gettysburg. Many historians believe it also marked the beginning of the end for the Confederacy.

Thirty years later, Chamberlain received a Congressional Medal of Honor for his conduct in the defense of Little Round Top. The citation read that he was awarded for "daring heroism and great tenacity in holding his position on the Little Round Top against repeated assaults, and carrying the advance position on the Great Round Top." Col. William C. Oates of the Fifteenth Alabama, who lost his brother John during those series of charges, strongly believed that if his regiment had been able to take Little Round Top, the Army of Northern Virginia might have won the battle, and possibly marched on to take Washington, D.C. He concluded philosophically that: "His [Chamberlain's] skill and persistency and the great bravery of his men saved Little Round Top and the Army of the Potomac from defeat... great events sometimes turn on comparatively small affairs."

Union Colonel Joshua Lawrence Chamberlain received a Medal of Honor for his extraordinary heroism on Little Round Top. Courtesy of the Library of Congress.

We finally came upon a small plaque that directed us to the spot where Chamberlain formed his defensive line, and we slowly made our way down a narrow path to the remnants of a line of earthworks. We couldn't help but feel a profound sense of respect as we stood in the footsteps of hundreds of brave soldiers who never made it off Little Round Top alive.

Instinctively, we began to canvass the area. My fellow investigator, Sean, immediately headed down the slope on which Confederate forces had relentlessly attempted their uphill attack. As darkness began to fall, I found myself sitting on a rock along the Union line, contemplating what it must have been like to be one of Chamberlain's men, facing a continuous onslaught of bullets. Two other investigators, Sean and Scott, were walking around taking temperature and electromagnetic energy readings.

"Very funny, guys!" Sean snapped suddenly.

I asked what in the heck he was talking about.

"Was that you, Scott?" Sean asked.

There was no answer, as Scott had walked back down the path toward the viewing station at the summit of the hill. Obviously, Sean believed Scott was trying to scare him.

Sean, now even more annoyed, continued, "That's just not cool."

I had to set the record straight. "Sean, Scott's not here, and I'm sitting about twenty yards above you on a rock along where the Union defensive line formed. What happened?"

"Are you serious?" asked Sean in an obvious state of excitement. "Somebody just walked right passed me and breezed by my left side. I saw a guy walk right toward me and I thought it was Scott. It had to be Scott."

Now he had my attention. "I'm coming down there. Don't move."

I moved quickly down the hill. As I hurried toward Sean, I heard the shuffling of leaves to my left, as if someone was scurrying along beside me … and then I heard rustling to my right. I stopped a few feet from Sean, becoming very still and observant. Sean stood frozen, as if paralyzed by some type of ray gun.

"Did you hear that?" I whispered.

"Yes ... loud and clear," said Sean. "What the hell was that?"

"I have no idea," I answered. "What did you see?"

I listened for more footfalls on the slope, but heard nothing.

"I was walking along slowly, trying to get a feel for what it must have looked like to the Confederates attacking uphill, when suddenly I saw the shadowy figure of a man—who at the time I thought was Scott—walking from that tree [points to his right] toward me," Sean started explaining. "I turned back around and suddenly felt as if somebody brushed up beside me, but there was nobody there. That's when I assumed Scott was trying to rattle me."

"Can you describe the figure?" I asked.

"The man looked to be about 5-foot-8, thin, and I could have sworn he was wearing a cap on his head," he continued. "Not like a cowboy hat or baseball cap, but more like a kepi or bummer. I couldn't make out a uniform, just the outline of the body and the small cap on his head. He was moving from right to left if you were watching from the bottom of the hill, and he was moving pretty fast."

This was getting good, so I continued to ask for details. "You felt him brush by you?"

"Yes, like a breeze, but definitely a tangible feeling of somebody whisking by me," explained Sean. "There was a real sense of urgency with this guy, like he was trying to get somewhere fast."

"Frantic, like during a battle maybe?"

"Exactly. Like he was running for his life, but I feel like my movements precipitated his movements, if that makes sense."

Union earthworks on Little Round Top at the time
of the battle. Courtesy of the Library of Congress.

I knew exactly what he meant, because when I rushed down the slope to get to him, we heard the shuffling on either side of me, like others were running alongside me. We stood for a few minutes, listening for any sounds, and straining to see in the low-light conditions. It soon became too dark, and we didn't have any equipment with us, so we decided to call it a night and check into our bed and breakfast. As we walked back up the hill, we saw Scott walking down the path toward us.

"This place is amazing," he said. "You can see a good portion of the battlefield from that viewing tower. Anything interesting happen here?"

Sean looked at me with a wry smile and said, "You have no idea, Scott."

As we left the battlefield, I wondered if the spirits of the soldiers who died there could react to our actions as if the battle was still in progress. If we made any sudden movements, for example, would they instinctually—as a result of having become emotionally attached to the location—spring into action, fighting on that hill as if it was still a hot afternoon in July 1863?

In order to understand how phenomena like this can occur, we must first examine a few of the basic laws of biology and thermodynamics. First and foremost, the fact that everything in the universe is energy has significant relevance as it applies to the possible existence of ghosts. Science has confirmed that energy exists everywhere and when in motion creates an energy field that allows energy to be absorbed, conducted, and transmitted. Our bodies radiate, absorb, and conduct frequency waves of energy, and each of our senses works through energies at specific frequency bands along the electromagnetic spectrum. Most surprisingly, if we magnify the cells, molecules, and atoms of which we're composed, we can see that at the most basic level we're made up of subtle energy fields containing little, if any, matter. We aren't merely physical and chemical structures, but beings composed of energy.

As such, let's look at the first law of thermodynamics, which is an expression of the principle of conservation of energy, which states that energy can be transformed (changed from one form to another), but cannot be created or destroyed. Based on these principles, we can now make an educated assumption that a transformation—not the destruction—of energy occurs at the time of physical death. At this point, the second law of thermodynamics takes effect. This law states that energy is dispersed from a core source and radiates outward in a symmetrical pattern until "acted upon." This happens as a consequence of the assumed randomness of molecular chaos, and it's also where the final pieces of the puzzle with regard to the creation of ghosts remain unidentified.

The second law dictates that upon death of the physical body, human energies generally disperse in a natural manner. This suggests that fragments of our conscious (or subconscious) thought can—at least for a while—interact with the surrounding environment in which bodily death occurred. What if this energy is "acted upon" in a way that either slows down or stops dispersal altogether? A traumatic death, for example, could create a "shock wave" that affects energy in such a way as to bind it to a specific time and place.

If you consider ghostly behavior, it makes sense. For the most part, haunting phenomena tend to be fragmented in nature. You hear footsteps, see a shadow out of the corner of your eye, or hear a disembodied voice calling out your name ... but whatever transpires only lasts momentarily. When sentient behavior manifests, it's as if the ghost is suffering from dementia or some stage of Alzheimer's disease. They exist in a haze, as if coherent thought is difficult. When you capture EVP, it's usually a sound, a word or two, or in rare instances a short sentence. Examples of EVP we've captured over the years include "cold," "mommy," a giggle, the rebel yell, a bouncing ball, and a gunshot. The most complete sentence we've ever captured was, "Won't you help me?" and the most compelling EVP I've ever heard from Gettysburg was, "I knew George Pickett." Truly profound, but only four words, not exactly the Gettysburg Address.

The bouncing ball and the gunshot can be categorized as residual in nature, but when a form of consciousness seems to be present and interaction of some kind occurs, we're left with more questions than answers. As it applies to what happened to us on Little Round Top, we can see how the scientific laws mentioned above might corroborate the existence of the shadowy figure and the rustling of the leaves on the ground.

Here's one explanation of what happened: On July 2, 1863, soldiers die on Little Round Top. Their deaths are traumatic in every sense of the word. When their physical bodies expire, their energy fields survive and transform, dispersing in a random way into the environment. Because of the emotional and sudden nature of the transformation, the last conscious thought gets stuck, thus remaining in the moment it was created just before bodily death. More than fourteen decades later, we arrive at Little Round Top and start walking around. One of these fragments of consciousness recognizes—on a purely instinctive and reactionary level—a man (Sean) walking down the slope of the hill. This particular energy field springs into action as if the battle is still raging, brushing past Sean as either a comrade in arms or mortal enemy. Sean sees the shadowy figure of a man and feels him brush by his shoulder, but then the event stops. Sean calls out, and I start walking down the hill toward him. Other energy fields present on the hill also react, following me down as if participating in Chamberlain's counterattack. I hear the rustling of leaves and twigs around me as I head down the hill. When I reach Sean, the ruckus around us stops. The paranormal event ends, and we leave the area having had our first paranormal experience at Gettysburg.

So what happened? Is it plausible that fragmented thought forms—which once existed in whole form as living, breathing human beings—still wander about the battlefield, reacting to their surroundings in a purely random and chaotic manner? This is only a theory, but a theory based in some part on accepted scientific laws. By simply continuing along a line of logic, you can easily come to the conclusion that, at the very least, consciousness survives death. What happens to us when we die can be debated, but the fact that we continue on in some form appears obvious to those who experience such events.

Day Three

July 3, 1863

ay Three of the Battle of Gettysburg would decide what direction the war would take. Either Confederate Gen. Robert E. Lee would defeat the newly appointed Commanding General of the Army of the Potomac, George Meade, or the North would withstand the South's final push and most likely secure the Union.

An eerie silence hung over the field; the dead scattered across the landscape. The silence was broken by the occasional shot from various Union sharpshooters on Cemetery Hill or Ziegler's Grove or from the Confederate sharpshooters in the town of Gettysburg and Bliss Farm. The constant moans of the wounded not yet removed from the battlefield were an underlying sound that the combatants had become numb to over the last two days of horrific fighting.

Lee had decided, against the advice of top commander Gen. James Longstreet, to attack the Union position where Gen. Ambrose Wright's brigade had penetrated and split the Union defenses on Cemetery Hill by the now famous Copse of Trees that became the guiding mark for Gen. George Pickett's Virginians, whose 6,000-strong division was fresh and had not seen any action yet. To Pickett's left would be Gen. James Pettigrew's division and Gen. Isaac Trimble's two brigades, and anchoring his right flank was Col. David Lang and Gen. Cadmus Wilcox's brigades. In all 15,000 Confederate soldiers would make the fabled charge. The other part of Lee's plan was to have his cavalry commander, Gen. J. E. B. Stuart, attack the rear of the Union line. Lee hoped that the combined effect would be like an anvil and hammer, crushing the Yankee defenders.

General Meade, having called a war council late in the night on July 2, had come to the conclusion that Lee would strike where he had penetrated his line on that day and so he made ready for a full frontal assault, knowing that the Rebels would have to go through "artillery hell" before even reaching his troops hunkered down behind the stone wall on Cemetery Ridge. On the backside of Cemetery Ridge he placed his reserves, with specific units behind them with the orders to shoot anyone who broke rank. The action started at three p.m. with a Confederate signal gun firing a single shot. The Confederate batteries along the line opened up, concentrating on the Bloody Angle and the Copse of Trees, trying to weaken the Union defensive line. The Union artillery answered, and for an hour and a half, more than 100 cannons blasted away at each other. The sound was so loud that people could hear the muffled noise in Washington, D. C.

Pickett started his advance at four, and by six p.m. the remnants of the once-invincible Confederate army streamed back to Seminary Ridge. The day would be costly for Lee, as the Union defenders sustained fewer casualties than the Confederates. Pickett alone had close to 2,600 of his men surrender on the field, and close to the wall lay more than 500 dead Confederate soldiers, most from Gen. Lewis Armistead's brigade. Armistead had crossed the wall at the Bloody Angle and led 200 Virginians up the slope of Cemetery Ridge. He was mortally wounded as he raised his hat on his sword near Cushing's Battery A, and 80 of the 200 men who followed him over the wall died there with him. On July 4, 1863, Lee would start his retreat South with what was left of his army later that evening.

The Battle of Gettysburg was over, and one of the greatest battles ever fought was now etched in history.

East Cavalry Hill

Chapter Twenty-One

Phantom Cavalry Retreat

— By Patrick Burke —

*O*n July 3, 1863, the third and final day of fighting in Gettysburg, Gen. James Ewell Brown "Jeb" Stuart's Confederate cavalry attempted to drive a dagger into the backs of the unsuspecting Union soldiers. Most people think of Pickett's Charge when they talk about the third day's action, but what's not so well known is the fact that Confederate Gen. Robert E. Lee had devised a more complex strategy to win the battle and capture most of the Army of the Potomac in the process.

As part of Lee's attack plan, Gen. Isaac Trimble's North Carolinians would strike the left flank and part of the center of the Union line on Cemetery Ridge while Gen. George Pickett's Virginians struck the center of the line. The extreme left and right flanks of the Confederate forces would demonstrate along their respective fronts to keep all of the Union forces focused away from the main thrust of the approaching rebels. Stuart was ordered to take his cavalry and strike the rear of the Union defenses, thereby disrupting their line of communications while Pickett and Trimble hammered them from the front.

Confederate Cavalry General J. E. B. Stuart, who attacked the extreme left of the Union line on the third and final day of the battle. Courtesy of the Library of Congress.

The plan was brilliant and aggressive, and it might have worked if it wasn't for an observant Union Gen. David Gregg, who heard cannon fire and caught sight of a company of Confederate cavalry. He rode close enough to see that it was a lead element of a much larger force. Indeed, Stuart's cavalry was heading toward the Third Pennsylvania Cavalry, which was set as a screen for the artillery reserve. Gregg quickly rode toward his commander's headquarters to alert him of the situation and get more cavalry support. While doing so, he came across two regiments of Union Gen. George Armstrong Custer's Michigan Brigade, which had recently been issued Spencer repeating rifles. These repeating rifles represented a significant tactical advantage during the Civil War, as they could fire twenty rounds per minute. Standard muzzle-loaders, on the other hand, could only fire two to three rounds per minute.

Custer was headed to the far left of the Union line as a screening force when Gregg approached and apprised him of the situation. At first Custer said he couldn't waver from his orders, but Gregg assured Custer he would take full responsibility for the action if he would only divert his brigade to aid the Third Pennsylvania. Custer finally agreed and arrived on the field just in time to join the gallant charge.

As Confederate Gen. Fitzhugh Lee (nephew of Robert E. Lee) led the Confederate charge, the Third Pennsylvania Cavalry smacked into the center flank of the rebel cavalry, and Custer drove his cavalry directly at the front of the column of Confederate troopers. "Come on, you Wolverines!" Custer shouted. Seven hundred men fought at point-blank range with Spencer carbine rifles, pistols, and sabers. The Confederates were eventually overwhelmed and forced to retreat.

I decided to visit this part of the battlefield for the first time in July 2006 with American Battlefield Ghost Hunter's Society team members Mike Hartness and John Burke. As the night progressed, a strange feeling came over John and me near the Michigan and Pennsylvania monuments. The energy was high and a sense of foreboding hung in the air. As we got closer to the Confederate positions, the energy began to feel muddy, more depressed than the normal "bring it on" energy I usually feel when confronted with Confederate spirits.

We stood by a road that splits the woods where Fitzhugh Lee initiated his charge and where the Confederate cannons were placed. The atmosphere was heavy, and we spoke in hushed tones—the rebel ghost soldiers obviously having a direct effect on us. As we walked along the road with the woods to our left (in a direction that would take us away from Custer's Michigan Brigade), we heard the sounds of walking and movement in the woods. We immediately stopped and listened closely as the commotion continued. It sounded like men and horses walking.

Mike walked over to the edge of the woods as John and I looked on. The sound grew fainter and finally stopped abruptly. When Mike came back, I asked him if he saw anything. He said no, but heard the sounds very clearly—men and horses moving away from the battlefield. Had we just experienced a residual haunting, hearing the imprinted energies of the actions that took place after Stuart's failed cavalry charge? Were the depressed feelings John and I felt those of the Confederates as they streamed back in defeat?

If you ever have the chance to go to the East Cavalry Field, you should do so. And when you're hanging out at the Michigan monument, ask the Union soldiers what they thought of Custer and if he was a hard commander. You might be surprised by the reply you get!

*Union Cavalry General George Armstrong Custer, who survived
the Civil War but met his violent end at the Battle of Little
Big Horn thirteen years later. Courtesy of the Library of Congress.*

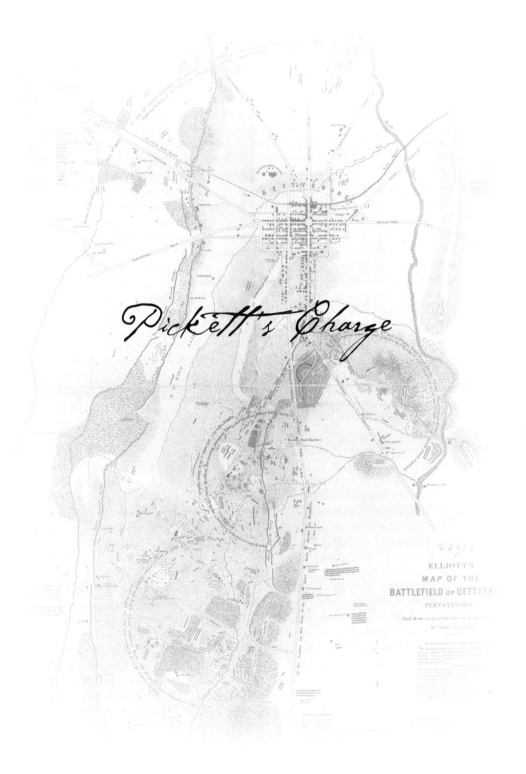

Pickett's Charge

ELLIOTT'S
MAP OF THE
BATTLEFIELD OF GETTYSBURG
PENNSYLVANIA

Made from an accurate Survey of the Field
by Transit and Chain

Chapter Twenty-Two

Pickett's Charge

— By Patrick Burke —

There are a number of times when we would just go and sit at the Bloody Angle, look across to Seminary Ridge and wonder what it must have been like. On our last visit, we planted ourselves on the wall and sat quietly listening for about fifteen minutes. I looked at Jack and said, "It's a strange feeling...I can feel the ghost soldiers all around us, but it's like they are waiting for something."

Jack nodded his head. "The calm before the storm."

I nodded in agreement, and then jumped at the sound of a single cannon firing.

"Holy shit!" Jack shouted. He asked if I heard the cannon firing.

I replied that not only did I hear it, but that just before I heard the sound, I saw a starburst of white energy erupt from the ground just off to our left.

Did we just experience the first cannon shot that opened the artillery barrage on Day Three of the fighting? Jack wanted me to ask a specific question based on what had just happened to us when I came out with the Double-Blind Ghost Box team, and I told him no problem.

Confederate General George Pickett led the main attack against the center of the Union line on the third and final day of battle. Courtesy of the Library of Congress.

During our Double-Blind Ghost Box investigation of Wright's brigade on Day Two of the battle (see chapter 11: A Study in Paranormal Archaeology), we had a moment when the ghost soldiers switched on us from Day Two action to Day Three action.

It happened near the forward position of Brown's Battery, when one minute we were talking to the ghost soldiers of Wright's brigade and the next minute Mary, who was standing near Dan and wasn't listening on the ghost box, said, "Layered history." Shawn, who had constantly been the Listener, stated that the ghost box was changing. He took off his headphones and I did the same. Shawn and Mary agreed that the vibration in the area was changing, a feeling that both Chris and I felt as well. I handed Mary the headset and asked her and Shawn to follow the direction the ghost box was taking them. Something was telling me that this was one of those rare times in an investigation when something completely unexpected was about to happen.

As with any haunting at a historical setting, you sometimes get what Jack and I call a "layered haunting" or "layered history." This happens when you have ghosts from different time periods trying to communicate at the same time. On battlefields, it can also happen when you're trying to communicate with the ghost soldiers from a specific time or date in a battle, but you may get ghost soldiers from a different action, different time, or different date. This is especially likely if the ground you're covering saw more than one engagement from different units on different days. This was exactly the case in this instance; I wanted to check on Wright's position coming up to Brown's guns on the second day's action, but the ghost soldiers wanted to jump into the third day's action.

Mary and Shawn were the listeners in the ghost box investigations as I asked for the location of the Third Georgia. I wanted to see if our pausing to make a change from me listening to Mary listening would stop the layering. Shawn started in immediately with a stream of replies, "Six thousand men got shot." Mary said the name "George" and I immediately asked if they were from Virginia. Dan quickly followed my question with his own, "Are you from Virginia?" Karen and Chris were still with us, and Karen, who isn't known for her sensitive abilities, said, "Yes. She got yes." Shawn continued, "I am an observer—Turned away—Confederates remain—Look forward!" Confederate Gen. George Pickett didn't advance with his division and instead stayed behind and watched the entire conflict from Seminary Ridge... as an observer.

I asked if the fighting at the wall was bad. This was the question that Jack had asked me to pose if we found that the ghost soldiers from Pickett's Division were active. "Desperate—Got 'em!" Dan asked how many men died and Mary and Shawn replied "607" and "The angle!—Gotta get outta here!—We're losing!—They shot him!" At this point I knew we had stepped into the firsthand recounting of Pickett's Division's fatal charge on the third day's fighting. Mary and Shawn both heard the name "Brume" and then Mary said "Eddie."

Was the final string of words that Shawn and Mary uttered the last words of the Confederate soldiers as they burst over the wall with Gen. Lewis Armistead? Imagine the hell these men must have been going through. Seeing the fleeing Union soldiers at the wall, the rebels must have felt a quick jubilation, perhaps thinking they broke the line. Suddenly they realize they're surrounded on three sides by Union infantry who are just pouring lead into them. Did we capture the last words of those brave men who jumped the wall? Let's recap what was said and how it relates to the actual battle:

"The angle!"—The Bloody Angle was where Armistead crossed the wall with about 200 Confederate soldiers.

"Gotta get outta here!"—Realizing that they had no support, they frantically looked for a way out.

"We're losing!"—The heart-wrenching realization that they weren't invincible and then the final straw ...

"They shot him!"—Armistead's men see him go down at Cushing's Battery and realize it's over.

In all our years of doing paranormal investigations and all of the solid evidence we've accumulated, nothing can compare to the moment when you realize you may have heard and captured the final words of men in desperate combat. Although this session wasn't in reference to why we were there, it was obvious that the ghost soldiers wanted their story heard and shared. We always feel a bit awed when we're honored by those who gave their last full measure when they share a moment in history with us. From the actual participants of the battle … incredible.

Town of Gettysburg

GETTYSBURG

ELLIOTT'S
MAP OF THE
BATTLEFIELD OF GETTYSBURG
PENNSYLVANIA

Chapter Twenty-Three

Within These Walls

— By Jack Roth —

Throughout this book, we've shared eyewitness testimony associated with Gettysburg hauntings. Many of these witnesses were visiting the battlefield at the time of their unexplained experiences. But what about those who currently work in the buildings that were inhabited in 1863? Some of the most compelling eyewitness testimony associated with paranormal activity in Gettysburg comes from the people who live and work in town. Many of the buildings that were witness to the battle still stand and are being used in various capacities. Quaint restaurants, bed and breakfasts, museums, and retail stores line the streets of Gettysburg, and the individuals who work in these buildings have many tales to tell.

What if you had repeated and daily contact with the vibratory energies associated with paranormal phenomena? Most people who come to Gettysburg are tourists and are there for only a few days, and yet every year, thousands of them experience paranormal activity. Imagine if you were in Gettysburg every day. How many ghostly encounters would you have? The real question becomes whether or not people can become more in tune with the specific frequencies associated with both residual and spirit energies due to a resonant familiarity that develops over time?

In scientific terms, resonance is an object or force getting in tune with another object or force. In her book, *The Resonance Key*, Marie Jones talks about how more scientists, as well as paranormal researchers, are looking at resonance as one possible explanatory hypothesis of the Theory of Everything. She states that "this comprehensive model may bridge the gaps between science and the supernatural, the normal and the paranormal, and go one step further to explain every facet of reality in between." This theory, she says, may indeed center on the vibratory nature of matter as it relates to both the natural and unnatural worlds, as well as on harmonics and sound, and furthermore, there are specific links between resonance and nearly every manner of mysterious phenomena reported.

Resonance, therefore, can result from constant or extended contact between two forces, thus allowing an individual to become more in tune with the specific vibrations associated with both residual and genuine spirit hauntings. Or, as Marie Jones suggests, can those things we call paranormal find shortcuts and routes to change the frequency of their vibratory nature until it is in phase, or in sync, with our own? Through resonance, a ghost soldier might lock into just the right frequency to show himself to a terrified tourist staying at a battlefield bed and breakfast.

Taking this line of thought further, using resonance, a ghost operating on a particular vibratory frequency might sync up with a similar frequency in our own brain, our consciousness, or perhaps even our environment, and, as Jones describes, manage to slip through the thin veil between worlds. Jones notes that ghostly apparitions are rarely consistent and are often described as "erratic" and "fuzzy." Some ghosts appear almost as three-dimensional projections, furthering the idea that the visual image is somehow being projected onto our reality from an alternate dimension.

Not surprisingly, almost every historic building in Gettysburg is reportedly haunted. Two in particular are currently open to the public as museums and also serve as the main events of a local ghost tour. Each property also has a tragic history associated with the battle and the collateral damage it caused. Not only are they both visited by thousands of tourists every year, they are also the workplaces to several tour guides and museum managers. As a result, they represent ideal laboratories for the collection of paranormal evidence and eyewitness testimony.

The Jennie Wade House

The story of Mary Virginia "Jennie" Wade is one of the most tragic of the entire Civil War. Jennie Wade was a twenty-year-old resident of Gettysburg engaged to be married to her childhood friend, Corp. Johnston H. Skelly of the Eighty-Seventh Pennsylvania. She worked as a seamstress with her mother, Mary, in their home on Breckenridge Street. To make ends meet, they also took care of a six-year-old boarder named Isaac.

For safety during the first day's battle, Jennie and her family moved to the brick home of Jennie's sister, Georgia Wade McClellan, on Baltimore Street. Jennie's sister had gone through a difficult birth about one hour before the Confederates rode into Gettysburg and needed to be cared for. As the battle escalated, the McClellan side of the house on Baltimore Street housed Jennie, her mother Mary, her brother Harry, her young boarder Isaac, her sister Georgia, and Georgia's newborn son. Although there was no heavy fighting in the area, a Federal picket line ran behind the house, and there was intermittent skirmishing between Union and Confederate sharpshooters who were hunkered down all over town.

Jennie spent most of July 1 distributing bread to Union soldiers and filling their canteens with water. By late afternoon on July 2, the bread was almost gone, and it was apparent that more would be needed the next day. Jennie and her mother left the yeast to rise until the next morning. At about seven a.m. on July 3, Confederate sharpshooters began firing at the north windows of the house. The prep work to bake biscuits began at eight a.m. At about eight thirty, while Jennie stood in the kitchen kneading dough, a Confederate musket ball smashed through a door on the north side of the house, pierced another door that led into the kitchen, and struck Jennie in the back beneath her left shoulder blade, embedding itself in her corset, killing her instantly. The cries of her sister and mother attracted Federal soldiers, who carried her body to the cellar. After the battle was over and the streets were once again safe, she was buried in Evergreen Cemetery in a coffin that Confederate soldiers had made for an officer.

Jennie Wade was the only civilian casualty of the Battle of Gettysburg. Unknown to Jennie at the time of her death, her fiancé Jack Skelly had been wounded and taken prisoner at the Battle of Winchester on May 13. Transferred to Virginia, he died in a hospital on July 12. News of his death came several days after the Southern army had withdrawn from Gettysburg. To add to the tragic nature of this story, their childhood friend, John Wesley Culp, who joined the Confederate army and talked to Jack as he lay mortally wounded in Winchester, was killed in action at Gettysburg on his cousin's farm before he could relay Jack's dying message to Jennie.

Today, the Jennie Wade House is one of the most popular tourist attractions in Gettysburg. The home, for the most part, remains historically intact, and visitors can see the actual hole in the kitchen door made by the rifle ball that killed Jennie. Several other bullet holes are clearly visible in the brick walls, as well as the damage caused by a misdirected 10-pounder Parrott artillery shell, likely fired from somewhere along Oak Ridge, two miles north of town. Over the years, people have seen apparitions of a young woman, a man, and several small children. The scents of rose perfume and freshly baked bread have been reported, and the sounds of sobbing, children laughing, and footfalls on the staircase have been heard. Also common is the sudden appearance of a ghostly mist, especially in the basement where family and friends kept vigil over Jennie's body until the battle ended.

During one of our weekend investigations of the battlefield, a couple (Frank and Cathy) clearly saw a white mist slowly appear in the basement while they were sitting on one of the benches. I interviewed them shortly afterwards.

"When did you first notice this mist forming?"

Frank began: "The rest of the group had already left the building, but we wanted to stay in the quiet of the basement for a few minutes. The story is so tragic, you just want to sit there and reflect. So we were sitting on the bench, and, Cathy, you actually saw it first."

"I looked up at where Jennie's body would have been wrapped on a bench, and to the right, in that corner of the room, I saw a white mist," added Cathy. "At first, I thought my eyes were just tired or something, but then I realized it was becoming more prominent. That's when I told Frank to look."

I asked Frank what he saw when he looked up.

"I was startled because it was clearly visible," he explained. "It was almost like smoke was coming out of a fireplace or something. But it wasn't smoke. We couldn't smell anything. It was just misty, but it was moving."

"How was it moving?" I asked.

Kind of like cigarette smoke," he said, "where some of the smoke is thicker than the rest, and just kind of wafting around. In no particular direction either. Just emanating from that corner of the room."

"Did you feel anything else? Cold spot? Warm spot?"

"Nothing," he said. "It just seemed so quiet. Like everything else just stopped. It was actually quite peaceful."

"Not that peaceful," Cathy interjected. "I mean, yeah, it wasn't menacing or anything, and it was really quiet, but it definitely wasn't normal, and it definitely felt like it was going to form into something."

"Like an apparition?"

"Yes," she said. "I was afraid that it would form into Jennie Wade."

"That would have been awesome," Frank said with a huge smile on his face.

I asked them what happened next.

"It just kind of faded away, and I have to say that I was just mesmerized and frozen with fear at that point," said Cathy. "If it would have continued to form into a figure, I would have run out of there. But it did just kind of disappear."

"Into the corner of the room?"

"No," she said. "Just dissipated."

Frank added that it just kind of faded out.

I asked if they took any pictures, but their cousin, who was also with our group, had their camera and had already left the house when the event occurred.

"So when it faded, you just walked out of the house?"

"We sat there for a few minutes trying to figure out what had just happened, but Cathy was spooked by it so we decided to slowly walk outside to tell you what we saw," said Frank. "It's a weird feeling when that happens. It really felt like everything else didn't exist at that moment. Just us and that mist."

Frank and Cathy are among hundreds of people who have had strange experiences while in the Jennie Wade House. Their experience with the ghostly mist was interesting to us because we already knew that other people had experienced the same thing in the same room, and the fact that there were two eyewitnesses to the same event makes it a corroborative sighting, which makes for solid evidence.

Soldiers National Museum (Orphanage)

One of the more emotional haunts of Gettysburg began when the body of a soldier was found on the Gettysburg battlefield tightly clutching a photo of his three young children. The small, glass-plate photograph turned out to be the only clue to his identity after he was killed. Freed from his frozen grip prior to his burial in an unknown soldier's grave, the ambrotype eventually found its way into the hands of John Francis Bourns, a Philadelphia physician who traveled to Gettysburg to treat wounded soldiers. After hearing the story of the unknown soldier, Bourns, whose intention was to "find this poor soul's family," recounted the story to the *Philadelphia*

Inquirer. The photo was printed in the *Inquirer* on October 19, 1863, with the headline, "Whose Father Was He?" The article read:

> After the Battle of Gettysburg, a Union soldier was found in a secluded spot on the field, where, wounded, he had laid himself down to die. In his hands, tightly clasped, was an ambrotype containing the portraits of three small children, and upon this picture his eyes, set in death, rested. The last object upon which the dying father looked was the image of his children, and as he silently gazed upon them his soul passed away. How touching! How solemn! What pen can describe the emotions of this patriot-father as he gazed upon these children, so soon to be made orphans? Wounded and alone, the din of battle still sounding in his ears, he lies down to die. His last thoughts and prayers are for his family. He has finished his work on earth; his last battle has been fought; he has freely given his life to his country; and now, while his life's blood is ebbing, he clasps in his hands the image of his children, and commending them to the God of the fatherless, rests his last lingering look upon them. It is earnestly desired that all papers in the country will draw attention to the discovery of this picture and its attendant circumstance so that, if possible, the family of the dead hero may come into possession of it. Of what inestimable value will it be to these poor children, proving, as it does, that the last thought of their dying father was for them, and them only.

Shortly after the *Philadelphia Inquirer* story, copies of the children's picture and related sheet music and poems cropped up across the North. They were sold with the intention of locating the man's family and supporting the orphaned children. Finally, in early November 1865, Philinda Humiston recognized the image as that of her children. She contacted Bourns, who returned the ambrotype and presented the widow with the profits from the sale of hundreds of copies.

The man whose dying act was to gaze upon the photo of his children was Sgt. Amos Humiston of the 154th New York Volunteer Infantry, a harness-maker from Portville, New York. He enlisted on September 24, 1862, shortly after President Abraham Lincoln issued a call for 300,000 three-year volunteers. During the next nine months, Humiston related his experiences to his wife, Philinda, in letters that expressed his longing for their family. Hoping to offer some solace, Philinda, in June 1863, sent him a sentimental keepsake, an ambrotype of their children, Frank, Frederick, and Alice.

"The likeness of the children pleased me more than anything you could have sent," he wrote in what would be his final letter. "How I want to see them and their mother is more than I can tell. I hope that we may all live to see each other again."

Amos Humiston's hopes were dashed by a Rebel bullet.

He was eventually laid to rest in Gettysburg National Cemetery, and in response to his heart-wrenching story, donations helped to found the National Soldier's Orphan Homestead in Gettysburg in 1866. Philinda accepted a position as the orphan's teacher and caretaker and brought her children to Gettysburg to live at the Homestead, which was less than a mile from where their father had died. During the battle, the building served as headquarters for Maj. Gen. Oliver O. Howard, the commander of the Union Eleventh Corps, and also as a haven for federal sharpshooters firing on Confederates who were hiding on the south side of town.

Philinda helped to raise over sixty children from eleven different states, but eventually, circumstances forced her to move away from the orphanage in 1870 and leave the children in the care of a younger woman named Rosa Carmichael. Unfortunately for the children, Rosa turned out to be a sadistic sociopath who beat the children, tortured them, tied them up in the basement for days, and even killed some of them.

Union soldier Amos Humiston was found dead on the battlefield, clutching a photo of his three small children. Courtesy of the Library of Congress.

The crimes were discovered after a runaway was caught and told of her experiences at the orphanage, which included being beaten by teenage boys who Rosa armed with sticks and being tied to a fence in the hot sun until she suffered serious burns. Everything the little girl said was later proved to be true as the house was investigated and found to be full of torture devices. The basement had even been converted into a dungeon where children were shackled to the walls and left to die. On June 11, 1876, Rosa Carmichael was arrested on a warrant charging cruelty to one of the orphans and held at $300. She was indicted on three counts of aggravated assault and battery, but in consideration of her sex, the court only sentenced her to pay a fine of $20 and the cost of prosecution.

This sentence only made her worse. She called upon the services of a brutal henchman, a boy about the age of nineteen who would beat and kick the little children to the delight and approval of the matron. In the bitter cold, she had a boy aged four or five penned in the outhouse. He was released at midnight by the intercession of two passing men who heard his screams. She also had a little girl stand on a desk in one position until she had to be lifted down, exhausted and helpless.

This controversy, along with charges of mismanagement and the violation of a trust fund, caused the closing of the orphanage by the county sheriff. The Homestead property was sold at a sheriff's sale during the summer of 1878, and the building was left vacant until 1950 when it became the Soldiers National Museum. Rosa Carmichael left Gettysburg, never to be seen or heard from again and never having to answer for her vicious crimes against the children. Today, the shackles can still be seen in the basement and many of the other artifacts are on display from that time period. Visitors often claim to hear children crying or feel invisible hands tugging on their clothes. Eyewitnesses also claim to feel the presence and see the apparition of an older woman, who, by all accounts, is as mean, nasty, and unpleasant as any living person they have ever come across.

One of the tour guides who works at the Soldiers National Museum told us a tragic story associated with the orphanage. One day, she said, one of the little boys in the orphanage escaped and ran off into town. He found himself at Gettysburg College in one of the girl's dormitories. A few of the girls who happened to see the boy decided to take him in from the cold.

By now, Rosa Carmichael had found out, and being the witch that she was, was not happy about it. She did a quick search of the town and found the most likely place he would go—one of the girls' dormitories. She searched each one and eventually came to the dormitory of the girls who had taken the boy in. They saw her coming and told the boy to hide out on the ledge outside their window. It was the dead of winter and frigid outside. The girls didn't think it would take long, but, unfortunately, it took a while because they were a little nervous and Rosa thought they were acting suspiciously. Eventually Rosa left, and the girls ran to the window and threw it open as fast as they could, but their hearts sank when they saw nothing. They checked the other ledges, the snow bank beneath the window, and the tree branches outside the window, but all proved fruitless.

Years later, another girl was studying alone in the same room when she had the feeling that somebody was watching her. She looked at the window and there was a young boy, his face and hands blue as if he had been in the cold too long, sitting on the ledge. She called to him, but he didn't respond. When she tried to get closer, he vanished. The tour guide told us that sightings of the spectral boy have continued to this day.

Kendra Marie Belgrad, a five-year resident of Gettysburg, lives not too far from the location where Amos Humiston was found clutching the photo of his children. She has worked for three years with Ghostly Images, the only tour company allowed inside the historical buildings known as the Orphanage (Soldiers National Museum) and the Jennie Wade House. As a tour guide, she imparts history and tells stories about the hauntings and previous visitors' paranormal experiences. She typically leads groups outdoors to a few locations around the buildings and then takes them inside. I was able to talk to her extensively about her personal experiences at these locations.

"How long did it take for you to begin having paranormal experiences at these locations?" I asked.

"Before I was allowed to lead tours, I had to follow a seasoned guide through the locations to learn the history and stories of previous experiences," she explained. "In both homes, it only took one trip through for me to notice there was something to the stories being told. I also worked during the day for a year in the Ghostly Images shop, the old library of the orphanage, and had some startling experiences."

"What was your belief in ghosts before you started working there?"

"I've always believed in the unseen," she admitted. "My earliest memories of the paranormal are from when I was seven. I know I wasn't scared when things happened. My mother told me that I behaved strangely from the time I could walk. I liked to play by myself as a child, but I do remember that my "imaginary friends" could move things or interact with me on a physical level. I don't think every bump in the night or unknown sound is a spirit. I always try to remain objective."

"Can you tell me about some of your earliest experiences?"

"I had quite a few paranormal experiences in Oregon, where I grew up," explained Kendra. "As I grew older I learned to keep many of them to myself. My father would always make fun of me because he didn't believe in such things, but my mother believed. She just didn't like being scared. I've seen people staring at me from second-floor windows of abandoned homes, while the people with me could only see curtains moving. I've heard voices when others didn't. Subtle things like when you feel something entering the room but can't see anything. You know they're there, you feel their presence, but in my case I don't always see them."

"Can you describe your first paranormal experience while working in these buildings?"

"At the Jennie Wade House, it happened as soon as I stepped through the front door," she said. "Being a trainee, I stayed to the back of the group and stood next to the front door after it was closed. Not long afterward, a sick feeling overcame me. My stomach began to clench and I thought I might faint, so I stepped away from the door. The feeling went away, but I noticed I had been standing in front of the door with the bullet hole, a stark reminder of a young girl's death."

I asked her what happened next.

"The group moved into the next room, the parlor, and I was jostled into the corner," she said. "Standing on the other side of the wall next to the spot where I originally felt bad, the sick feeling returned. I thought I wasn't going to make it through the tour. The guide saw my discomfort and allowed everyone to look around the room, spreading us out. When I stepped away from the corner, the feeling left me again. These two spots weren't the only places in this house where I felt physically ill, but they were the first."

"Why do you think that happened?"

"When the energy has been very strong, be it from spirits or electricity, I've gotten sick," she explained. "These two areas at the Jennie Wade House continue to make many people ill."

I asked her about her experiences at the Orphanage.

Kendra began, "My first experience there wasn't very nice. The tour guide motioned us into the building and I closed the door. I once again stood at the back of the group, allowing others to be first when moving through the room. Usually before something physically happens to me, I'll feel a tingling sensation up the back of my neck. It's almost like an alarm that alerts me to something close by. Well, my neck began to tingle as a pain flared up in my right shoulder. It felt like someone was digging their knuckle into my skin and twisting it back and forth."

"What did you think might be happening?"

"I thought perhaps it was a muscle spasm, though I had never had anything like this happen before," she said. "I tried to roll my shoulder and massage it with my left hand but it didn't help. The tingling in my neck increased and I spoke aloud in a low voice, 'Stop it.' The sensation stopped instantly. A woman standing next to me quickly said 'Sorry' and, with a strange look on her face, moved away."

"Did the tour continue at that point?"

"The group went down into the cellar shortly after and I found a seat at the back of the room," Kendra explained. "My back was against the stone foundation. As the guide spoke about the haunting, I felt the skin on my hands and knees begin to tingle. I didn't know if this was paranormal or not, but I hadn't experienced this before and thought it would stop quickly, when something began digging into my shoulder again. I had read somewhere about negative spirits not liking the flash of a camera because it reminded them of the 'white light.' With my camera raised above my shoulder, I snapped off several pictures. Instantly the pain was gone again."

"Did the tour guide notice?"

"The guide saw what I did and gave me a strange look, but continued with her tour," she said. "When she allowed the group to mill about, she quietly asked me why I took a picture of the wall. I told her I was trying to stop something from happening, and she responded with, 'You felt a pain in your shoulder, a digging.' I was amazed and said that I had. She told me I would be a guide in the Orphanage because all the guides who worked there were greeted by the negative spirits this way."

I thought it was pretty brave that they still became guides after that.

Kendra said that someone didn't like her and was trying to scare her away, but it didn't work. I thought to myself that they raise tough stock in Gettysburg. I asked what else had she experienced at the Jennie Wade House.

She said that in early May 2011, she and two other guides took a young man and his chaperone through the Orphanage and Jennie Wade House on a private tour. It was a quiet night at the Orphanage, so they moved on to the Jennie Wade House. Toward the end of the investigation, the young man said he left his backpack in the parlor on the Wade side of the house, so she volunteered to lead him back through to retrieve it while the others waited outside. When they reached the second floor and stepped through the wall that separates the duplex, their trifield meters began to indicate there was energy in the room.

They took a few moments to see if anything else would happen. As they stood in the bedroom just above the stairs to the kitchen where Jennie died, they both saw a black shadow cross the room and disappear down the stairs. They quickly followed and when they reached the landing we both saw a ball of bright white light hovering above the floor. It began to swirl in a circular pattern.

Kendra didn't want it to disappear before she got a closer look, so she jumped from the landing just in time to see it go through a cupboard door in the pantry. It was quick, but it was also very real. They both laughed because there was nothing else to do but be happy that they saw this activity—actual energy moving about the room. The young man wanted to see something amazing and luckily she was with him when he did.

"How about other experiences in the Orphanage?" I asked.

"Last year I had just finished a tour and I was standing at the doorway to the entrance of the Soldiers Museum," she began explaining. "I was talking to two of my guests and noticed that I didn't have my lantern. They told me I'd left it in the cellar, so I thanked them, closed the door, then turned to walk to the back of the room where the stairs lead to the cellar. Halfway back, I walked through the most disgusting smell. It was so rancid that I gagged, then raced past to get to the stairs. Before I could get to the doorway of the cellar, I heard a loud sound behind me. I was the only person in the room and couldn't see what could have made the noise. Picking up the pace, I raced down the stairs and grabbed my lantern, said thank you to the children and told them not to follow me home. I quickly walked back out and, in the same spot, smelled the wretched scent again."

"Did you go through in your head what it could have been?"

"I was trying to think of logical explanations," she said. "Did a sewer line break? Maybe someone had horrible gas before they left, but could it linger that long? Was there something rotting in the garbage basket? I told my manager and his wife about the smell, and he asked me if anyone on the tour had smelled it while in the cellar. When I said no, he walked over to the spot but couldn't smell anything. I walked over to the spot, and it was still there!"

"So you were smelling this awful stench and they couldn't smell anything?"

"Yes," Kendra replied. "After literally gagging, I asked them why they couldn't smell the rotten eggs and rancid smell of rot. They said they couldn't smell a thing. Incensed, I walked to the spot again, waited for my manager's wife to pass, and hollered for her to stop. I said, 'It's right here! You can't tell me you don't smell this. It's awful!' She stopped in her tracks, looked around the room, and then looked at me in a most serious manner. She asked, 'Kendra, do you want me to tell you what you smell?' I said yes. Her manner was very serious as she told me how, a year before, they had a psychic medium enter the building. He stopped at the door and said there was a young man in the back of the room. He described a teenage boy with a stick in his hand glaring at him. The boy was dressed like someone who would live in the orphanage—checkered shirt, woolen pants. The medium tried to approach the boy, but when he got halfway to him, he gagged and said the boy smelled awful. He described the smell just as I had."

"So the medium is the only other one who smelled what you did?"

"Yes…and the manager's wife was there that night, and she watched the medium become sick in exactly the same spot where I stopped her," she explained. "Chills went up my spine, because in all my life I had never smelled a spirit before. I wasn't so happy when they started to tease me and told me that I had a new fan. I didn't want that smelly boy following me around."

"The medium's description of the boy matches with the history of the building, correct?"

Definitely. It makes sense that he was probably one of the boys Rosa would have beat the children and do her dirty work," she stated. "He is obviously a very mean spirit. I have to say this wasn't my favorite encounter."

I asked Kendra of all the experiences she has had, which one was the scariest.

"After working and living in Gettysburg for the past five years, I don't scare easily," she said. "With that being said, there was one experience where I wasn't able to stand still. In early April 2012, an investigative group came to town to do a taping of the Orphanage and the Jennie Wade House. I was one of the guides that assisted them in the house and helped with their investigation later in the evening. At about three a.m., two of the team members, both women, asked me to go down into the cellar of the Jennie Wade House with them while the men went to the second floor. We were going to conduct an EVP session to see if we could record any activity."

"What kind of equipment did they have?"

She described that several cameras had been set up around the room and the lights and power to the building were off. One investigator sat at the front of the room with dowsing rods and the other sat in the middle of the room with a night vision camera pointed at the first investigator. They began to conduct a Q&A session with the dowsing rods and recorders. Because they were in the dark, the investigator with the night-vision camera would tell them what the rods were doing.

Kendra's job was to move around the back of the room with an energy meter and record energy fluctuations. As the investigators asked questions, she leaned against the wall near an opening that connects the two cellars in the house. She heard several noises in the other room, so she pushed aside the sheer black curtain that covers the doorway and reached her hand in. The meter suddenly shot up to its highest reading. Kendra alerted the investigators, and they started asking questions of James Wade, Jennie's father, because it's believed he frequents that section of the cellar. But the high energy reading went away, so essentially whatever was there was gone. She stuck the meter back in, and to her surprise it fluctuated again, but this time something else happened. A white mist curled at the end of the meter, covered the lights and then obscured her hand. Her hand disappeared before her own eyes, covered in what looked like a thick smoke-like substance.

I asked what she did next.

"That was it for me," she exclaimed. "I panicked. I said a choice word and scared the two investigators as I quickly backed across the room. The investigator with the dowsing rods called out to me and asked if I was okay. I needed a moment to gather my thoughts, but then I explained what had happened."

The lady with the dowsing rod immediately started questioning James Wade. She wanted to know if he had tried to scare me. She then asked me to move to the front of the room where she sat. Her plan was to coax the spirit out further. I sat down beside her, and she asked if the spirit wanted them to leave. The investigator with the night-vision camera suddenly felt a deep chill envelop her and also felt something brush her shoulder, as if someone had bumped her as they walked by. It was at this point Kendra felt it was time to take a break.

"I can laugh about it now," Kendra said, "but not at the time."

I asked her if she ever captured an EVP at these locations.

"Many voices have been heard, both on tape and with the naked ear," she said. "Sometimes they sound like small children laughing or crying. Other times they sound more sinister, like growls or moans. One recording was captured in the old dining hall in the Orphanage. You can hear me talking about the history, but someone talks over my voice. The first sounds like a man muttering, but you can't understand what he's saying. The second voice is clearly of a woman telling me to 'Go to hell!'"

That's disconcerting, I thought to myself.

"I know things like this should scare me, but voices don't do any harm," Kendra continued. "I'm more intrigued as to why I would be damned to hell. Was it something I said?"

"You have a great attitude about this stuff, which is important considering you're around it all the time," I told her. "In your opinion, why do you think these locations are haunted?"

"I believe there are many different factors," she explained. "The bricks used to build a lot of the historic buildings in Gettysburg contain quartz and limestone. Some investigators believe these minerals act as a charge to power residual hauntings. The minerals are found all over town and the surrounding ground. Perhaps the tragedies that occurred within the walls of each building have anchored the spirits within. They aren't trapped at the location, but their belief that they can't leave this plane of existence keeps them near a place they once knew or called home. Belief is a very powerful force."

I told her that she had an acute sense of ghostly phenomena and what it could be.

Kendra continued her with her impressive response: "I'm familiar with the difference between what investigators define as a residual haunting and an intelligent haunting. I believe humans have a tendency to try and define what they don't understand, whether the definition is correct or not. Perhaps a residual haunting is really an intelligent spirit stuck in a loop and not what we think of as a repeating pattern alone. The living may never truly know why spirits do what they do, unless these spirits decide to explain it. Trying to understand human behavior and define it in a specific pattern has been a challenge for scientists throughout our existence. Spirits were once living humans, which makes it more difficult to guess their motives now that they are dead."

"I agree," I told her. "Again, you have a very objective, open attitude about this. When you think about the possibility that the spirits of children are roaming or trapped in the Orphanage, how does that make you feel?"

"When I first heard the story of the Orphanage, I was saddened," she admitted. "I know spirits linger, but children lost and alone really struck a chord with me. However, after being in the building interacting with the activity and seeing the childlike behavior within, I know most of the time these children are happy."

"Really?"

"Yes," she said with certainty. "For most of them, this was the only home they ever knew. For a time, their joy was taken from them and bad things occurred, but now, with so many guests visiting them, I believe the children are happier than they have ever been. Why would they leave when guests come to see them every night? These people bring them toys and candy, and listen to their stories. They have a captive audience that come out to see them and play. I believe that as long as they have someone who remembers them, they will always feel as though they're at home."

"Do you think the spirit of Jennie Wade still resides in Gettysburg?"

"It's definitely possible," she said. "We humans have a tendency to return to the locations where monumental moments in our lives occurred. A woman, short in stature and dressed in Civil War attire has been seen with two young men also dressed as reenactors near Culp's farm. This farm isn't far from the house where she died. They always get everyone's attention because they look so authentic, but if a picture is taken they don't show up on it. Sometimes they fade before a photo can be taken. Could that be Jenny, Jack Skelly, and John Culp? Maybe, but we'll probably never know for sure."

"How have these experiences changed you as a person? Do you consider yourself more spiritual? More in tune with other realms? More skeptical? Less afraid of the unknown?"

"They've made me more considerate of those who have died," she explained. "Whether it's a soldier who lost his life on the field of battle or the children who may never leave the Orphanage, I have to live with their presence and teach others to do the same. We can't traipse around this earth expecting others to do what we wish; we can only ask and not be angry if they don't comply. That goes for the spirits as well. I've always believed in them and always will because I trust my own senses. I'm more afraid of the living than I am of the dead, but the fear of the unknown is always there. Perhaps that's what truly keeps us on our toes."

I talked to Kendra about living and working in Gettysburg, and the fact that she's around these energies every day. She either knowingly or unknowingly interacts with them on a pretty regular basis. I asked her if she thought that she had tuned into some of these energies, and vice versa, as a result of this constant contact.

"Absolutely," she stated. "Different people have told me that a little boy at the Orphanage is always hanging around me. I've felt this before, but because I can't see him, I can only guess that this is the case. But I look at it this way … these spirit energies were once living energies, and as living beings we are constantly connecting with each other. We are attracted to some people more than others for many reasons, so why would this be any different if that same energy still exists after death? Yes. I think that for all of us who live and work in Gettysburg, we have become connected to many of the energies that exist here as a result of the battle and its aftermath, but I'm definitely okay with that."

My interview with Kendra was enlightening for many reasons. First and foremost, I appreciated her objective and open-minded approach to the paranormal activity that surrounds her. I was also impressed with her knowledge of paranormal theory, which is a testament to her desire to acquire knowledge regarding what she and others around her are experiencing. Perhaps most intriguing was her comfortable acceptance that she has probably "gotten in tune" with certain energies as a result of her familiarity with them, even though she can't quantify it. Although we can't know for certain that resonance is playing an important role in the activity that Gettysburg residents and employees are experiencing, it does provide some peace of mind. After all, if the spirits of soldiers, women, and children are roaming the battlefield, streets, and hallways of Gettysburg, it's comforting to know that they can connect with the living and perhaps feel a sense of love, caring, and belonging from those open-minded enough to acknowledge their presence.

Well, maybe not Rosa Carmichael.

Afterword

Control.

It's a word scientists love, and an environment they demand when conducting research. Laboratories offer the most controlled environments, as parapsychologist and paranormal research pioneer J. B. Rhine and his team proved when they conducted successful extrasensory perception (ESP) experiments at Duke University in the 1920s and 1930s. Rhine's experimentation led to reliable analysis due to the replication of his observations. To this day, ESP is the only paranormal occurrence to which some scientists will acquiesce, in large part due to Rhine's efforts.

Unfortunately, most paranormal phenomena dictate that researchers and investigators leave the comfortable confines of the laboratory and venture out into the field. This, after all, is where the action is. A wise man once said that if you want to catch fish, go where the fish are. The same principle applies to ghosts, as only so much can be gleaned from ghostly phenomena in a laboratory.

The problem: Too many unknown variables taint evidence, rendering it useless to those who subscribe to the scientific method. The scientific method demands observation, hypothesis, experimentation, analysis, conclusion, and theory. In the field, it's often difficult to cover the stages of scientific rigor in the few seconds an anomaly might occur, and you can't go back and make it happen again on demand (lack of repeatability). Spirits don't keep schedules, and emotional imprints can't be bottled up for laboratory analysis—at least not yet.

Having said this, some of the most active and challenging places to conduct paranormal research are battlefields. These historic landmarks have presented difficult challenges to field researchers. Some of these hindrances include natural elements associated with the outdoors such as rain, wind, and extreme temperatures, which all can affect electronic equipment, film stock, and an investigator's fortitude. Indigenous animals can make it difficult to conduct electronic voice phenomena (EVP) experiments, as the sounds they make can be easily misinterpreted as paranormal.

And then there are people. Millions of tourists visit battlefields every year. During the course of any given day, dozens of school buses drop off children of all ages to explore these hallowed grounds. At Gettysburg, some of these kids tend to run around Devil's Den like it's a Chuck E. Cheese's. It's important that children experience these places, but it's a nightmare for field researchers!

Large battlefields such as Gettysburg cover more than ten square miles, and strange anomalies have been experienced on just about every portion of it. Remember, the larger the area in which you conduct an experiment, the less control you have over outside elements. Lugging around hundreds of pounds of equipment over long distances is no walk in the park. Storing equipment, keeping it safe, and having appropriate power sources in the middle of a battlefield can be a tricky proposition when the nearest shelter or power source is hundreds of yards, or even miles, away.

Topography also adds to the chaos. Battlefields are covered with trees, bushes, logs, leaves, and rocks—a perfect environment in which to see a thousand faces on Mars! Remember, the mind creates familiarity out of chaos (simulacra), so in a place like Gettysburg, every photograph can conceivably have a blurry tree or moss-covered rock in the background that will look like a soldier once the mind connects the dots.

Adding to these headaches are time and money. Some battlefield parks have banker's hours, so your time may be limited once it gets dark. Unless you want to spend time in county lockup, you need to take the time to secure the appropriate permits, or permission, depending on where you go. Also, traveling costs money, whether you travel by car (gas), airplane (ticket expenses), or horse and buggy (time away from work!). Field investigators traverse long distances in order to "go where the fish are." Such research can be likened to expeditions that require planning and smart logistical execution.

Although these obstacles can be daunting, there are things you can do to make your battlefield investigation a success. For example, always pick smaller areas in which to conduct experiments. Remember, you have more control the smaller your "outdoor laboratory." In Gettysburg, we narrow our experiments to specific parts of the battlefield. On the twenty-six-acre Wheatfield, for example, we conduct a grid-like walkthrough with several participants. These investigators walk across the field at twenty yards apart holding handheld equipment such as cameras, tape recorders, and trifield meters. Simultaneously, we set up video cameras on higher elevations that offer wide-angle views of the entire field. The result—several people with possible psi abilities being documented exploring every inch of the field while holding environmental monitoring equipment.

As mentioned above, battlefields are covered with trees, bushes, tall grass, dead logs, and rocks. At various angles, these objects can look like soldiers, horses, and other battlefield objects. In order to document locations properly, always shoot a series of photos to create a panoramic view of the entire area from where you stand. By doing so, you cover every angle and can better determine if that bearded Union soldier is actually a jagged rock with fungus and moss growing on it. Another effective way to decrease the chances of misinterpretation is by setting up a triangulated coverage with video equipment. Triangulation is an approach to data analysis that synthesizes data from multiple sources. By having multiple video sources in which to view various angles of Devil's Den, for example, we can rule out a false positive by viewing the ghostly image from another angle and determining it's only a rock that happens to looks like a man's face from one particular angle. Triangulation can also help corroborate something as being paranormal in nature if more than one camera picks up the same anomaly.

In the end, field investigations are imperative to paranormal research. Rhine proved certain phenomena could be observed and replicated in a laboratory. Some of the more unpredictable phenomena, however, cannot. Therefore, interaction with the environments where these events occur is necessary. Environmental factors that are geographically specific such as electromagnetic field anomalies, family dynamics, and traumatic historical events seem to play a role in various types of hauntings, so being in the trenches can yield the best evidence as it applies to the effects of these variables. Importantly, interviewing eyewitnesses where the phenomena occur—not in a parapsychologist's office or laboratory—seems to be the best way to extract accurate testimony due to familiar triggers in the environment. As field researchers, we can put forth due diligence in order to gather acceptable evidence, especially if, over long periods of time, we can establish trends that give scientists something to attempt to replicate either in the field or in a laboratory.

We intend for this book to be the first in a collaborative series that documents compelling evidence collected on battlefields across the world. Our goal is to accumulate a body of evidence that compels other researchers and scientists to recognize the importance of battlefields as they apply to paranormal research.

Life happens "out there," and that's where we need to be in order to find the elusive answers to life's most puzzling enigmas. Our experiences at Gettysburg have taught us that exploring the unknown represents an unparalleled adventure and that investigating battlefields results in a clearer understanding of both historical events and the specific sacrifices associated with war that make them the most horrific, yet enduring, of all human experiences.

Appendix A:
History of Paranormal Research

Since the dawn of primitive cultures, human beings have questioned what happens when they die. The idea of "spirit" goes back to early man, who became consciously aware of his mortality and wanted to know if getting mauled by a sabertoothed tiger represented his finite end. Consciousness gone. Kaput. Nothingness.

In 1871, England's first professor of anthropology, Edward Burnett Tylor, published *Primitive Cultures*. In it, Tylor explains the theory of "animism," which he defines as the belief in spiritual beings. According to Tylor, the belief in spirit began with early man's attempt to explain basic bodily and mental conditions such as sleeping, waking, trance, or other unconscious states, dreams, illness, and death. He believed that primitive man pondered these things and developed the idea of a soul or spirit separate from the body, which was then extended to animals, plants, inanimate objects, heavenly bodies, and deceased ancestors.

This led to primitive faiths, which in turn led to spiritual rituals. Some early cultures began to believe that the spirit wanders away from the body during periods of unconsciousness such as sleep, or that after death the spirit lingers near the body of the dead person. It was a common practice of groups holding such beliefs to pacify the ghosts of the dead by offering food, clothing, and other objects these spirits might find useful in the afterlife. These types of rituals still exist in many cultures today. In fact, the practices of ancestor worship and the mourning rites of many modern civilizations most likely originated in this newfound belief in the spirit world.

As civilizations and technology developed, however, it was no longer acceptable for people to simply believe in ghosts. Scientists and skeptics began to question how exactly it was that spirits existed, and of course, whether this could be proven scientifically. These inquiring minds focused on psychic phenomena, or psi, which refers to events that appear to contradict physical laws and suggest the ability to send or receive messages without the use of the five senses. These processes include extrasensory perception (ESP), the acquisition of information without using the known senses. ESP is comprised of telepathy, the transfer of information from one person to another without using any of the known channels of sensory communication; clairvoyance, the acquisition of information about places, objects, or events without the mediation of any of the known senses; and precognition, the acquisition of information about a future incident that couldn't be anticipated through any known related process. Along the same lines as precognition is retrocognition, the purported abstract transfer of information about a past occurrence. Another fascinating manifestation of psi is psychokinesis, which is the direct influence of mind on physical objects or events without the intervention of any known physical force.

The organized, scientific investigation of paranormal phenomena officially began with the founding of the Society for Psychical Research in London in 1882. It was the first organization established to examine these abnormal occurrences using scientific principles. In its early days, the SPR focused on the explosion of "extravagant paranormal claims... related to the spread of the new religion of Spiritualism." The American Society for

Psychical Research was founded a short time later in 1885. Its mission has been "to explore extraordinary or as yet unexplained phenomena that have been called psychic or paranormal, and their implications for our understanding of consciousness, the universe, and the nature of existence."

In 1927, the pioneer of contemporary parapsychology, Joseph Banks Rhine, founded the parapsychology lab at Duke University and began his seminal extrasensory perception (ESP) experiments. He coined the word "parapsychology," the actual discipline that seeks to investigate the existence and causes of both psychic abilities and life after death using the scientific method. Due to Rhine's somewhat successful mental-telepathy experiments, the great majority of psychical studies in the last fifty years have occurred in laboratories and focused on ESP. You see, in order for something to be deemed "scientific" and worthy of study in the scientific community, it must be observable, empirical, measurable, and repeatable. Most metaphysical incidents don't comply with scientific protocols, but Rhine's experimental methods held the promise of supplying repeatable demonstrations. This has been a mixed blessing, because although psi research creates a pathway to understanding the human mind, the repetitive forced-choice procedures studied in laboratories fail to capture the kinds of ghostly experiences people report in everyday life. They also preclude consciousness-after-death possibilities.

This conundrum brings up the obvious question: How does ESP tie into ghostly encounters, if at all? Are ghosts manifestations of our psychic abilities, or can spirits of the dead (souls) actually manifest themselves in our earthly realm in tangible ways? Either way, the sobering truth remains that after more than a hundred years of research conducted by some of the most brilliant minds on the planet, we're no closer to understanding the nature of spirit than our sabertooth-dodging brethren. However, in recent years, the growing number of paranormal researchers willing to leave the confines of the laboratory and venture out into the field where the real action occurs has yielded a strong body of evidence in favor of the existence of various types of ghostly peculiarities.

Appendix B:
Gettysburg's Quantum Quirks

For some, experiencing Gettysburg can be likened to peering down the proverbial rabbit hole. Energy vortices captured on film and video, strange wave-like ripples in the atmosphere seen with the naked eye, high electro- and geomagnetic readings garnered from high-tech equipment, and other strange anomalies experienced on almost every portion of the battlefield. But what do these highly unfamiliar events represent?

Extensive volumes have been written regarding the relationship between paranormal phenomena and the nontraditional scientific possibilities that might validate them as part of the natural and known universe. Quantum physics explores the realities of life at the subatomic levels, and this has had consequences in terms of our own consciousness and experience, as well as our relationship to the universe around us. Quantum theory suggests there are interconnections and influences between subject and object, which, according to traditional scientific theory, cannot exist. This opens the door to alternative explanations of consciousness and challenges us to explore them with an open-mindedness that goes against a societal belief system still entrenched in superstition, fear, and skepticism.

As it relates to Gettysburg, how might quantum physics explain the paranormal phenomena encountered there on a regular basis? How can a man see the "imprint" of a Union regiment marching near the Wheatfield more than a century earlier? How can a video camera capture a ghost soldier jumping over a fence at the Triangular Field? How can we hear the sounds of battles already fought? Can we experience history firsthand, as a result of some universal law of physics scientists haven't discovered yet?

For more than a century, the greatest minds on this planet have studied paranormal phenomena and their implications on our understanding of the universe and human consciousness. Theories associated with time slips or time warps can be traced to Albert Einstein, who proposed the theory that time and space form a continuum that bends, folds, or warps from the observer's point of view, relative to such factors as movement or gravitation. A time slip, therefore, might be a perceived discontinuity in time, either one that allows something to travel backward or forward in time, or an area of space that appears to travel through time at a different rate from the rest of the universe. If we assume these discontinuities are possible, it might explain how a couple who visited the Gettysburg battlefield in 1989 reportedly had a conversation with a barefoot, emaciated, sweat-soaked man dressed in a filthy, ripped, gray uniform who politely asked for a drink of water, then slowly disappeared before their eyes!

Mathematical developments associated with the superstring theory, considered by some scientists to be the most outrageous theory ever proposed, may help theoretical physicists explain encounters with the past as well. Research suggests that disruptions and warps can occur naturally in space, resulting infrequently in theoretically possible random time events. These warps or disruptions might allow for any action or event to transcend time and space—and be seen, heard, or felt at any point in time. Superstring theory attempts to explain all of the particles and fundamental forces of nature in one theory, or a Theory of Everything. The implications of superstring physics are radically changing our ideas about the nature of space, opening up the possibility that extra dimensions, rips in the fabric of space, and parallel universes actually exist.

Theoretical physicists also are excited about the existence of the zero-point field (ZPF), which may explain how everything that exists in the universe is connected to everything else. The ZPF is made up of zero-point energy (ZPE), virtual particles whose electromagnetic fluctuations fill every corner of space and are never at a state of absolute zero momentum, but instead vibrate at the most minute rate of oscillation allowable by the laws of quantum physics. Marie Jones, in her book titled *PSIence: How New Discoveries in Quantum Physics and New Science May Explain the Existence of Paranormal Phenomena*, describes this vibration as "a tiny, residual jiggle." Jones explains that by virtue of the ZPF, reality is one big spider web with an infinite number of fine strands crisscrossing, intersecting, and creating a wholeness that extends throughout time and space.

What implications do the existence of the ZPF and ZPE have on the validity of residual hauntings? According to Jones, the supposed recording of the energy of an event could take place in the ZPF, which can be compared to the Akashic Records of Edgar Cayce, upon which every memory, action, thought, and thing was written. These imprints, or recordings, could have found a way to exist intact upon the ZPF, and those who see replays of past events could have found a way to tap into them. As a result, psychically inclined individuals may smell gunpowder, hear cannon fire, and see flashes of gunfire while walking around Little Round Top, Culp's Hill, or Devil's Den.

Theoretical physicists remain very busy in laboratories seeking answers to these quantum enigmas, and paranormal field investigators continue to attempt to document tangible evidence at places like Gettysburg that can help validate these theories as they relate to hauntings. For field researchers, it's figuring out exactly what they need to be looking for and what tools they should be using that remains the challenge.

Paranormal investigators such as Joshua Warren, author and president of LEMUR (League of Energy Materialization and Unexplained Phenomena Research), approach paranormal field research in such a way as to best contribute to scientific inquiry. Warren's goal is to accumulate well-documented cases and create a database of hard evidence. "If ghosts are non-physical entities that aren't restricted to the known laws of physical matter," he supposes, "then by using the scientific method and creating a collective database, we may one day have enough data to isolate the patterns and correlations that will finally realize the essential conditions for spectral interactions to occur."

Obtaining this type of hard evidence requires taking as many environmental readings as possible when conducting field research. In fact, a basic arsenal of field equipment might include geomagnetic field meters, electromagnetic field meters, temperature gauges, ion detectors, and more. Given the strange atmospheric conditions that seem to manifest when witnesses experience imprint hauntings and time slips, it seems only prudent to follow the advice of Warren and other serious investigators—go to great lengths to measure environmental conditions in an attempt to isolate the patterns and correlations associated with these phenomena.

When conducting paranormal investigations, however, the best opportunities often occur when you least expect them, which is why being prepared at all times remains critical to the success of field research. For example, about five years ago while doing a field investigation at Gettysburg, a team psychic appeared very excited as she approached us in the Wheatfield. She said a portal had opened up in the Rose Woods (adjacent to the Wheatfield), but that she couldn't find me in time before it closed. Apparently, her psychic abilities enable her to see these portals appear, and she describes them as a disruption or ripple in the atmosphere. It's during these brief moments that she feels it would be most advantageous to take environmental readings and photographs because this is when paranormal activity "peeks through our dimensional veil."

We immediately thought it would be a great idea to walk around the battlefield with her—for hours or even days if necessary—until this phenomenon occurred again. It seems well worth the effort to be able to measure the particular vibrations, frequencies, or electromagnetic fluctuations associated with these anomalies. We consider her experience a profound one and are still deeply disappointed we weren't in her general vicinity when this supposed portal opened.

These portals may very well represent the "rip in the fabric of space," the discontinuity in time, the warps or disruptions associated with superstring theory, or the manifestation of the zero-point field. And if one or more of these theories do apply to the phenomena reported at Gettysburg, what came first, the rabbit or the hole? Gettysburg may be located on or around an energy vortex or other cosmic quirk, thus exacerbating the frequency of hauntings in the area, and the battle itself may have created the strong emotional imprints that somehow allow these quantum doors and windows to open up more frequently.

We can't know for sure at this point, but our combined intuition tells us that whatever this psychic detected was very important, and somehow these ripples in the atmosphere are the key to explaining at least some of the paranormal phenomena documented at Gettysburg and other battlefields across the globe. The answer is there, in front of us; we just need to know how to tap into its source, or essence.

Appendix C:
Field Investigation Tips

Throughout this book, we have documented firsthand accounts and photographic evidence while also discussing theoretical possibilities pertaining to paranormal phenomena experienced in and around Gettysburg and its historic battlefield. We hope you have learned a thing or two about this mysterious and beautiful place, and we also encourage you to get out there and go to haunted locations to perform well-executed investigations that will yield viable results for the good of the entire research community.

Having said this, paranormal field investigators should remain cognizant of the following when investigating haunted locations such as Gettysburg:

- **Keep an open mind regarding quantum theory and the general laws of physics.** You don't have to be a physicist to be a good paranormal investigator, but you should read the equivalent of *Quantum Physics 101* (see Appendix B) in order to gain a basic understanding of the physical laws of the universe and how they might relate to paranormal phenomena.

- **Bring a broad array of environmental measuring tools,** including geomagnetic field meters, electromagnetic field meters, temperature gauges, humidity gauges, barometric pressure gauges, radiometers, ion detectors, etc. These tools will help you document baseline readings and record any anomalous deviations from those baseline readings.

- **Document every small detail of the landscape in question.** Note the topography including rock types and formations (Devil's Den), and take latitude, longitude, and elevation readings (Little Round Top) to create an accurate grid of the area being investigated. These topographical details might play a role in triggering the phenomena. Be sure to document by taking plenty of still photographs.

- **Research as many cases regarding residual hauntings as possible in order to create a model on which to build an investigative strategy.** For example, many imprint hauntings are preceded by a palpable change in atmosphere. By knowing what to look—and feel—for, you can be prepared when environmental fluctuations occur.

- **Understand that consciousness plays a factor in these phenomena;** therefore, it's important to utilize a good medium and/or sensitive during field investigations in order to localize paranormal energies and document the effects these environments have on certain individuals.

- **Interview eyewitnesses beforehand in order to determine optimal focus areas.** For example, many incidents at Gettysburg that fit the profile for imprint hauntings occur in the Triangular Field. Knowing this, you should focus on conducting particular experiments and taking specific readings in this area. Compiling a lot of documentation at a specific location can be beneficial to future research.

- **Ask experts in particular disciplines for ideas on what they might want documented at a particular location or investigation.** By doing so, you can accumulate data that is potentially beneficial to other researchers moving forward. It will also help you develop strong investigative techniques and protocols, and you will end up with solid research as a result.

- **Make sure you have a well-balanced team.** Your field-investigation team should include a team leader who makes sure the team stays on task and has the historical research on hand to help direct the investigation, a sensitive, an equipment/tech person, a photographer, and a documenter, whose job it is to take copious notes and collect all of the field data. We also suggest bringing along a second sensitive; the two of them can help validate and enhance the information being obtained by one another.

- **Share your research with others!** In order to make progress in any area of study, a clearinghouse of information must be made available to all researchers. The sharing of thoughts and ideas is the fastest way to enlightenment.

In the end, all we can do as paranormal field researchers is use our investigative skills, our intuition, and the proper equipment to best obtain and document a body of evidence that may someday assist physicists, psychologists and other scientists as they attempt to answer life's most profound questions. Gettysburg provides the perfect "outdoor laboratory" in which to do this.

The Civil War-era American poet Nathaniel Hawthorne once wrote, "Our Creator would never have made such lovely days and have given us the deep hearts to enjoy them, above and beyond all thought, unless we were meant to be immortal."

We believe, as did Hawthorne, that human beings are innately aware of something metaphysical, something highly abstract that exists beyond the physical world (in which we only exist temporarily). Humanity's quest for knowledge underscores this awareness. As it applies to paranormal research on battlefields, we owe it to ourselves and the millions of ghost soldiers around the world to optimize the knowledge that can be gleaned from the etchings of their heroic sacrifices, respect those sacrifices, and enjoy the journey of exploration along the way.

Recommended Reading

Gettysburg, by Harry W. Pfanz

Gettysburg—The Second Day, by Harry W. Pfanz

Gettysburg, by Stephen W. Sears

Landscape Turned Red: The Battle of Antietam, by Stephen W. Sears

American Heritage Battle Maps of the Civil War, *edited by* Richard O'Shea

The Gettysburg Then & Now Companion, by William A. Frassanito

A Strange and Blighted Land: Gettysburg, The Aftermath of a Battle, by Gregory A. Coco

Three Days at Gettysburg: Essays on Confederate and Union Leadership, edited by Gary W. Gallagher

The Killer Angels: The Classic Novel on the Civil War, by Michael Shaara

The Last Full Measure: A Novel of the Civil War, by Jeff Shaara

Stars in Their Courses: The Gettysburg Campaign, by Shelby Foote

Hallowed Ground: A Walk at Gettysburg, by James McPherson

This Hallowed Ground: A History of the Civil War, by Bruce Catton

When the Smoke Cleared at Gettysburg, by George Sheldon

Early Photography at Gettysburg, by William A. Frassanito

The Wheatfield at Gettysburg: A Walking Tour, by Jay Jorgensen

Lost Children of the Battlefield: A Collection of Photographs Found at Gettysburg, from the collection of Professor J. Howard Wert

Blue-Eyed Child of Fortune: The Civil War Letters of Colonel Robert Gould Shaw, edited by Russell Duncan